Praise for *Me, My Bike and a Street Dog Called Lucy*

Who saved whom? Ishbel is a truly incredible and determined woman whose emotional story takes you on a journey of tears, laughter, hope and inspiration with her heart-warming friendship with a stray dog that becomes a connection and rescue for both of them. Beyond inspiring!

Dion Leonard, author of *Finding Gobi*

An incredible story about amazing Ishbel and her cycling adventure. Ishbel takes us on her rollercoaster of a journey through life, and through Turkey, on a bike with Lucy. It's a great read – particularly if you're a cycle tourist or dog lover.

Simon Stanforth, founder of Stanforth Bikes

'Hooked by page 2. Tears by page 5. This is a gem of a story written by a brave and inspiring young woman with an XXL heart. If you love travel and love animals, you'll adore this book.'

Jason Lewis, author and explorer

'I've enjoyed following Ishbel's travels over the years – she has such a wonderful way with storytelling. Down to earth, honest, funny – she mixes grit with unshakable optimism. Her passion to explore this precious planet under her own steam is infectious, and it's a joy to be swept up in her world, and in ⸱

love most about this book, however,

the dark times. She shines a light on the many twists and turns one woman's life can take, and how ultimately she has turned her own often raw and painful experiences into a force for good in the world. That is the greatest triumph of all, and I have no doubt that her story will inspire millions.'

Anna McNuff, adventurer and speaker

Dear Sue,
G8 meeting you in
Edinburgh!

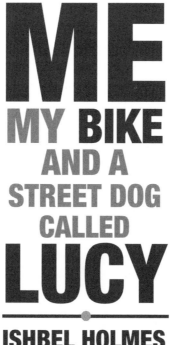

ME
MY BIKE
AND A
STREET DOG
CALLED
LUCY

ISHBEL HOLMES

Ishbel Holmes

x

First edition published August 2018
Bradt Travel Guides Ltd
IDC House, The Vale, Chalfont St Peter, Bucks SL9 9RZ, England
www.bradtguides.com

ISBN: 978 1 78477 607 7 (print)
e-ISBN: 978 1 78477 560 5 (e-pub)
e-ISBN: 978 1 78477 461 5 (mobi)

British Library Cataloguing in Publication Data
A catalogue record for this book is available from the British Library

Photographs
Front cover
Photo of Ishbel © Ishbel Holmes
Photo of Lucy © Jane Akatay
Back cover and colour section photos © Ishbel Holmes

Typeset by Ian Spick, Bradt Travel Guides
Production managed by Jellyfish Print Solutions; printed in the UK
Digital conversion by www.dataworks.co.in

CONTENTS

FOREWORD
by Jan Rees

*M*e, *My Bike and a Street Dog Called Lucy* is an extraordinary story about the union of an independent, adventurous woman and a fiercely determined dog.

Ishbel's story is a poignant insight into a young woman's physical and psychological journey across Turkey and through the reflections of her traumatised past. Her ambition was to cycle the world alone and perhaps to prove to herself that she needed no-one but herself to survive. What she encountered was the unlikely companionship of a street dog, Lucy. And what she saw was a reflection of herself – an innocent victim of terror, abuse and rejection. Both had experienced trauma. Both had learnt not to trust. Yet the power of basic human–animal instinct and nature brought them together.

Saving Lucy required a six-hundred-kilometre detour from Ishbel's path, on a cycle with a makeshift basket to carry her. The story depicts their moments of creativity, uncertainty, hope, despair and sheer determination. Ultimately it reveals the strength of the relationship and bond that they developed and the power of reciprocal healing.

Sadly Ishbel's story is not an unusual one. She entered foster care at 16 years and ran away from her first carers. Like many other looked-after children her 'care' became a series of displacements and transitions. In England there are currently over 72,000 children in care. Research shows us that instability for children (multiple changes of family, school, social workers, etc.) can lead to vulnerability of exclusion, exploitation and abuse (Children's Commissioner Stability Index 2018).

Having been an adopter of two boys and fostering many children over the years I came to realise that many of those young people inevitably find themselves navigating the traumas of their past in adult life. The dilemma is that so many have no family support or limited social capital and, like Ishbel, find themselves alone.

My belief has always been that there is a therapeutic value in bringing people together who have had similar experiences. And this is something that Rees Foundation (A Charity for Care Experience People) hosts in the form of Peer Networking Events. Ishbel attended one of those events in 2017. It was the first time she had spoken to another care leaver since leaving care some 20 years earlier! For her it was liberating and life-changing. She discovered that by opening up about her experiences she not only helped her peers to articulate their emotions and perspectives, but she helped herself too.

Just as Ishbel was enthused by the charity I founded, I have been inspired to facilitate adventure treks for other care experienced people. This is the power of reciprocation!

This book is a testament to Ishbel's resilience. I believe her story will resonate with many and give a candid insight to others, enabling a wider audience to have a realistic understanding of a person's journey through care and beyond. My hope is that it will facilitate innovation and creativity around ways of helping care-experienced people to build positive and meaningful relationships.

Jan Rees, OBE
Founder of Rees Foundation
2018

A HERO OF MINE
by Frank Gilhooley

To say I am proud to be Ishbel's friend is a colossal understatement. She is a hero for womankind, for selflessness and for survival. She is a hero of mine.

I have been blessed to work with extraordinary and vibrant human beings from all over the planet, and none do I admire more than Ishbel Holmes.

Her journey from literal abandonment as a juvenile to World Bike Girl is astonishing, and in this beautifully crafted book we see how the courage of one woman shines through after a childhood of incredible hardship.

Ishbel is indeed a hero, because she has overcome hurdles I could only face in my worst nightmares.

When I chat with her, the conversation regularly ends up on a topic which is as important to any human as the food we eat and the air we breathe... the subject of love.

There is a beautiful and fascinating aspect of a dog's nature that transcends the common trade-off in so many of our human relationships, and it is this...

... a dog's love is unconditional.

There is a painful but beautiful moment in the book that touches my heart deeply as Ishbel, alone in a foreign country, sees her new-found canine friend being savaged by a pack of wild dogs. She is transported immediately back to one of the most vile and painful moments of her childhood, and we understand exactly what is occurring deep inside her soul. A choice must be made. She makes a life-changing choice there and then.

There is a fantastic saying that I believe should be carved in tall stone pillars for all to see:

'Opportunity is always waiting to be found, buried in the rubble of your past.'

Ishbel set off on a journey, looking for the opportunity to find something that had been missing from her past. Something pure and true and authentic, that she could rely on.

Her beautiful and inspiring book is a true and passionate journey of one woman looking for the unconditional love that had been missing for her entire life.

For Lucy
I'll love you until the day I die.

CHAPTER 1

On my very first night cycling the world, with 30 kilos of luggage hanging from my bicycle, I realised I had forgotten to pack a lighter. I sat outside my tent in darkness, striking two pebbles together without success. Crawling into my sleeping bag that night, I was hungry and disappointed, knowing a *real* adventurer would have found a way to light her stove and cook dinner.

Five months later and pedalling across my tenth country, Turkey, I still yearned for the day I'd resemble an adventurer, but to date I'd had too many hysterical moments involving spiders, slugs, and imaginary monsters to count myself as the real deal. Each night I wild camped, and every sunset brought along with it my three biggest fears: one, that human beings would find me and murder me; two, that animals would find me and eat me; and three, that a combine harvester wouldn't see my tent and I'd be combine-harvested up.

I'd wanted to build a campfire many times along the way through Europe, but visions of burning down whole forests had stopped me. I had entered Turkey through Greece just over a week ago and today I was about 200 kilometres west of Istanbul, cycling a quiet coastal road along the Sea of Marmara. The empty winter beaches scattered with driftwood were inspiring me once more, and I decided that tonight, yes, I would build the first campfire of my trip. I smiled – one step closer to being a real adventurer!

It was late afternoon as I turned down a road to my right, leading me through a cluster of wooden houses and towards a beach. I stopped at a small village shop, which was dusty and packed full of everything you could possibly need, from DIY supplies to cans of fruit; everything but customers.

Money was tight, and I deliberated greatly before buying an onion. I would cook that with tonight's pasta, adding my remaining garlic to give it more taste. Only last week I had been down to my last twenty quid when a Scottish company, Intelligent Data Group, saw my Facebook post declaring my plan to dumpster dive and donated some cash to keep me going. The less I spent of it, the more days ahead I could eat. This struggle was nothing new. I had always travelled on a shoestring budget. I figured not having money was a small inconvenience for the priceless experiences that travelling by bicycle brought.

I found the beach empty except for a few dogs in the distance. The winter-grey sea and boarded-up tourist beach huts gave it an abandoned, derelict look. Although it was perfect for building a campfire, I had an uneasy feeling I could not shake. As a woman cycling the world on my own, I obeyed my instincts. Disappointed, I turned back to cycle the way I'd come, with intentions of trying the next beach along.

I took a final glance behind, hoping it would provide the thumbs-up I needed to stay and build my campfire there. Instead, I was greeted by the surprise of a light-coloured dog padding along to the rear of my bicycle. I grinned. During my past days of racing bicycles, we were taught to ride in what's called the 'blind spot' of the competitor in front; this tactic allowed us to remain hidden while conserving energy. This dog was absolutely nailing my blind spot!

I knew it was best not to acknowledge or feed random dogs along my route. They could try to tag along, which was an impossible situation for both parties. Other cycle tourers had warned me, 'Remember, you're cycling the world; stray dogs are not your problem!'

I ignored the dog and cycled back through the village and onto the main road, vacant of traffic. I checked behind. The dog was still there. Pushing on the pedals, I blasted away as only a pure sprinter can, a human machine of fast-twitch muscles designed for power and speed. I glanced behind once more. The dog was running after me as fast as it could, trying to hold its position. I noticed its moving shape was odd – the dog was definitely limping.

I kept on, faster and faster, repeating the mantra, 'I'm cycling the world and stray dogs are not my problem!' A long, gentle downhill ensued, which was enough to give me the extra speed I needed. The dog fell behind. Another glance to the rear, and I could still make out its shape, now just a small dot in the distance. For the love of God, why was it still running? Give up, I pleaded silently to it. Give up.

A voice within me, starting out as a whisper but then silently screaming until it could not be ignored, cried, 'Ishbel, this is wrong! What you are doing is wrong!' I pulled the brake levers and stopped. Turning around, I waited, hoping the dog wouldn't reach me. If it did, I would just have to deal with the situation I found myself in. Eventually the dog arrived, panting hard, and dropped to the ground a metre or so away. I held out my hand as an offering of peace and spoke softly. It kept its distance. This dog confused me. I hadn't spoken to it or given it food. I hadn't even acknowledged it. Why would it chase me so hard and for so long, and then refuse even to come near me? This dog was a weirdo.

I let the dog rest a few minutes and then began wheeling my bike along the road, unsure what to do next. The dog followed behind. I rolled my eyes. Building my campfire like a real adventurer would have to wait another day; instead, I would camp here, in the sloping field.

The deep, rippling furrows of soil, which farm machinery had prepared for planting, made it difficult terrain for a fully loaded bicycle. Putting my head down and ignoring the pain in my shoulders, I pressed against the handlebars and used all my body weight to push the bike onward, until I could move forward no more. With no hedgerows, the dirt field lay exposed to the road, and I hoped I was far enough away that people in passing cars wouldn't notice me camping in the night.

The dog lay in the earth and watched me from a distance as I pitched my tent. I watched her back as I waited for my pasta to boil. She was a female, so thin her bones stuck out. One of her paws was deformed, and I wondered what had happened to it. Why did she limp? Was she in pain? She had a pink plastic circle in her ear. I wondered what it was. Maybe it was from her family, like a dog-collar tag in Britain. If she did have a family, I didn't like them much because they didn't look after her. But then I remembered that some people in Turkey struggled to feed their own children.

I felt bad for her, but I didn't know how I could help. I ate half the pasta and held out the rest for her to eat. Still she refused to come near. I left the pot on the ground some distance away. Jesus. Even a starving dog wouldn't eat my cooking.

My thoughts drifted to my ex-boyfriend and how we had laughed when I declared I didn't need to be good in the kitchen when my bedroom skills were so good. No matter how much I tried not to think about him, I always did. Before committing to this idea of riding the world, I had asked him if we could try again, and with a broken heart I'd accepted that we couldn't. He had begun university to progress his career and said he didn't trust himself not to fail if I walked out a second time declaring I didn't love him.

He had a point. We had fallen completely, madly in love, and I had reacted by finding lots of things wrong with him that needed changing. He had tried hard, but I went on to destroy our relationship with excruciating brilliance. What I had done made no sense at all.

I finally figured out that I was too damaged to love or be loved. And with that awareness came determination and a certainty that I could change.

Tidying up after dinner, I emptied the uneaten pasta into a rubbish bag. The dog was still watching my every movement. Once I moved away, she went over to the open bag and began eating. I felt even sadder for her.

It grew dark, and I was tired. I spoke a few gentle words of good night to the dog, climbed inside my tent, and zipped it closed. I felt the warmth of my sleeping bag and immediately felt guilty. Pushing away thoughts of fleas, I unzipped the tent and began patting the ground to invite her in. She didn't budge. I sighed and zipped myself back in. I was glad she had eaten, but I hoped she would be gone when I woke up. There was no way this dog was coming with me.

When I awoke the next morning, my first thought was, 'I hope the dog's gone.' In fact, it was more than a hope. I prayed she wasn't there as I put on yesterday's clothes in the tiny space that was my one-person tent. She wouldn't be there, no way. She had been petrified of me.

Unzipping the tent, I hunched my way out into the early morning sunshine. There was the dog, lying beside the rubbish bag. This wasn't good.

'Hello girl!' I mustered a cheery call, hiding my disappointment. She moved farther away. Why on earth did she hang around when she was so scared of me?

Not knowing what best to do, I stood scanning the farmland, spying only a country road and a scattering of farmhouses in the distance. I thought about the village where she had joined me. She was painfully thin and obviously had some past injuries, and yet she had somehow managed to survive. I decided I would take her back to the beach where she had begun following me. Perhaps the tag in her ear was from her family and I could find them around there. Or maybe someone would recognise her and claim her. There was no other option. Coming with me was out of the question. I was cycling the world.

I ate some bread and offered her a piece, but she refused, so I threw it at the rubbish bag and sure enough she gobbled it up. I packed up and slowly pushed the bicycle back over the ploughed field with the dog following behind. We reached the desolate tarmac road and I cycled slowly so that the dog could keep up, glancing behind to make sure she was OK. I had no idea why she limped, and I didn't want to put her through unnecessary pain.

We arrived back at the village and the dog moved out in front, which gave me hope that she thought this was home. Angry barking came from a field on my right, and suddenly four dogs ran out across the road. I shouted out, but they reached her and attacked all at once. To my horror, the dog didn't run. She didn't fight back. She just lay down. She just lay down and accepted what was happening – the dogs snapping at her injured hip and leg with sharp teeth bared and saliva flying.

In that moment, I was transported back to being 16 years old in the back of a car, in a moment when I didn't fight back. I hadn't cared enough to fight back. For months before, I'd lain in bed every night, silently screaming, sometimes punching the pillow but mostly punching myself. My face was swollen and red from tears as I promised God or the universe or whoever was in charge of the world that I'd be a good girl if I could just have my family back. But no matter how much I promised, nothing changed. I was on my own, in foster care, surrounded by strangers and far away from home. That night in that car, I eventually stopped saying no and simply stared out the window into darkness, grateful to be punished finally for being so horrible that my own mum didn't want me.

I threw down my bicycle and ran screaming toward the dogs with a force I'd never known. I kicked and pulled at the snarling animals, screaming until they ran away. She was lying on her side, and I knelt down, tears filling my eyes. She moved her head just enough to lick my hand. Her big, chocolate-brown eyes looked into mine and melted my heart. I told her she was a good girl, and in that moment I named her Lucy.

Looking her over, I couldn't see any wounds. I stood up and walked a few paces away with my back to her, tears rolling down my face. Why had she just lain there? Why hadn't she run? Why hadn't I run all those years ago? I scolded myself and angrily wiped the tears from my face. Lucy didn't need my tears, she needed my help. Just as I had needed help years ago – help that never came. Taking a few deep breaths, I crouched down beside her. I smiled and patted her, telling her softly that everything was going to be OK.

As I stood up, so did Lucy, and she nuzzled into my leg. Together, we walked the bike to the village shop that I'd visited the day before. I told Lucy to wait outside with my bicycle, and then laughed at myself. How would she even understand me? Not only was she a dog and I human; she was Turkish and I was British. Yet somehow, talking to her seemed to bring us closer.

The elderly shop owner was happy to see me again and began chatting away, not bothered that I understood nothing. I tried to explain to him about the dog outside. He didn't comprehend. I took him outside and pointed to Lucy. He smiled, nodding his head, and then disappeared back inside the shop. He reappeared, throwing bread to Lucy. My heart warmed. What a lovely man. Then he motioned for me to cycle away while she was distracted by eating the bread. I said no, that I wanted to make sure she was OK. He nodded that he understood, but to my shock he began running toward Lucy, waving his hands and shouting at her. She ran away as fast as she could. He looked back at me, pleased for helping, but I was horrified. I said goodbye and thank you in one breath and got on my bike, cycling in the direction she had run, desperate to see her again. But she was gone. I finally turned around, consumed by an overwhelming sadness, and pedalled slowly back to the main road. Well, it was better this way, I thought.

I was just putting my foot on my pedal to accelerate when... movement. I looked back, and there was Lucy running as fast as she could across the village toward me. Watching her distorted shape pound ever closer gave me a rush of absolute joy. I got off the bike. Kneeling down, I stretched out my arms and waited for her with a big smile on my face. She reached me with such force that she almost knocked me over, and I scooped her into my arms, telling her over and over what a good girl she was.

CHAPTER 2

I had no idea what to do next. But leaving Lucy for more dogs to attack her was not an option. I had mobile reception, and thankfully Google was on hand to rescue me from my own ignorance.

My search brought up a website in English about stray dogs in Turkey. I dialled the number and an English woman answered, 'Hello, Samantha speaking.' I could not believe my luck.

'Hello, my name's Ishbel and I'm cycling the world.'

I hesitated, realising I had no idea what to say next.

'You're who… you're what?'

'I'm Ishbel. I'm in Turkey. I got this number on your website. I've got a dog. She began following me. She's on her own.'

Silence.

I stammered on. 'I was wondering what people did with dogs in Turkey.'

'What do you mean?' she asked in an incredulous tone.

'Well, what do people do with dogs wandering around? She's just wandering around on her own. She's got a pink tag on her ear. It has the word *Gönen* and a number on it. I think Gönen is the name of her family.'

'What are you talking about?' Still the incredulous tone.

'The dog. She has a pink tag on her ear,' I repeated. 'I think it's from her family, but I don't know how to find them. Is there somewhere I can take her to help find her family?'

'That tag in her ear means she's a street dog.'

'Oh.' My heart fell.

Samantha went on: 'And it means that you are in Turkey's Gönen region.'

My face reddened.

'She has no family then?' I asked.

'No.' her voice was getting higher in pitch. 'She's a street dog. The ears are tagged to show the dogs have been neutered and vaccinated against rabies, and then they are returned to live on the street.'

'How awful,' I exclaimed.

Silence.

'Well, what should I do with this one?' I asked.

'There are millions of street dogs in Turkey,' she said dryly.

'Yes, but what should I do with this one? She's walking funny and was attacked by dogs. I can't just leave her.'

She paused, and then finally said, 'Look, if you get this dog to me, I'll give her a place at my sanctuary.'

The word *sanctuary* filled my imagination, and I thought of London's Covent Garden spa. In Britain, sanctuary meant luxury, and I couldn't believe our luck. This was definitely a day I should buy a lottery ticket.

'She will be fed and cared for, and all the dogs run free on my property.'

'Thank you so much!' I was flooded with excitement. 'Where are you?'

'Muğla.'

'Great, where's that?'

'About five hundred and fifty kilometres south from where you are right now.'

'Five hundred and fifty kilometres?' My excitement shattered. 'But that's impossible. I'm on a bicycle. Isn't there somewhere here I can take her to?' I was crushed.

'No!' She suddenly sounded very forceful. 'Whatever you do, do *not* take her to a shelter! You are taking her to die. It's different here than in Britain. They will put her in a small cage, she won't get out, and she will die quickly. If you get her to me, I promise you she will have a place for the rest of her life in my sanctuary.'

I thanked her again, and the call ended with Samantha repeating not to take Lucy to a shelter. As I hung up, the words *but I'm on a bicycle* rang in my ears. I looked down tenderly at Lucy. She has no home. She has no family. Just like me. And suddenly I was crying.

I thought back to how I'd begun my world cycling adventure in Nice, on the French Riviera. I'm not French, but rather was born in England to a Scottish mother and Iranian father. The majority of my life was spent in Scotland, a nation equally excited by the prospects of a sunny day as by winning the lottery (both highly unlikely). Yet I chose to start out in Nice. I told people with a big smile that I was fed up with the Scottish rain and wanted to enjoy my first kilometres in sunshine. And I'd believed it too, even as I boarded a cheap flight to the south of France. But now, watching Lucy lying next to my bicycle, alone and unwanted, I suddenly became aware of things missing from my departure that other adventurers had in their blogs: that night-before farewell dinner with loved ones, ending in nightcaps and hugs; scenes of setting off, those first pedal strokes surrounded by cheering family; parents holding back tears; and the overwhelming emotions of leaving all that is familiar behind. All that is home. Looking at Lucy now, I had an awful realisation: my bike ride began in the sun not to avoid the rain, but to avoid the horrible empty pedal strokes of the first kilometres of a world tour with no home to cycle from and no family to see me off.

I knew the reality of being alone in the world, of being discarded by family and society to a life on the streets. Lucy was injured, she had just been attacked, she was vulnerable and on her own and unable to protect herself from harm. But even though I knew one hand reaching out could change everything for Lucy, there was simply no way I could transport her 550 kilometres. I was on a bicycle. It was impossible.

Andre, a drunk German I'd met in Italy some months before, popped into my head. I'd been pedalling toward Venice and it was early morning as I cycled past a couple of drunks on a park bench. Realising I was going the wrong way, I turned back, passing them once more. This time I noticed the touring bicycle beside them and was stopped by my curiosity.

Andre's face was a bright lobster red, and his words were slurred. My first thought was that he was in desperate need of a wash, which showed how bad he was because it had been nine days since my own last shower. He explained he was from East Germany and that his trip had begun long before the Berlin Wall came down. In fact, he declared he'd been cycling the world for 30 years. I at first dismissed the 30-year claim as a consequence of the empty bottle beside him. But as Andre's stories continued, coupled with his ability to speak multiple languages, I realised he could well be the real deal. I had heard tales of cycle tourers like him, but so far they had been only invisible legends.

Andre had a small white dog called Sweet whose home was a green plastic crate attached to the handlebars over his bike's front wheel. A pink plastic hood that looked like it belonged on a doll carriage was fixed over the top, offering Sweet protection from sun and rain, and his toys and bowls hung from different points around the bike.

That thought brought me immediately back to reality. That was it! I had to find a way to put Lucy on the bicycle just as Andre had done with Sweet. Sure, Lucy was a big dog and Sweet had been small, but I had left to cycle the world as one of the fastest female cyclists in Scotland and Iran, and I had to believe that such a pedalling pedigree would help me find a way to save Lucy. Still, the prospect of fitting a 20-kilo dog on my already loaded bicycle and then actually cycling it made me want to laugh. It was impossible – wasn't it?

I began walking the bicycle and Lucy toward the next town, which I thought might offer more opportunities for a solution. Since the dog attack, Lucy remained close by my side, but each time a truck approached from either direction, she threw herself off the side of the road and lay flat on her belly, not moving until the noise of the truck was gone. There was no exception to this, and I imagined a truck had caused some of the damage to her body. A wheel rolling over her paw made sense given its deformed shape. God, that must have hurt.

I arrived at the outskirts of a town called Biga and stopped at what looked like a hardware shop. Knowing only a few words of Turkish, all I could do was motion for the shop assistant to come outside.

Even though I travel the world, I am at a loss with languages. When the Iranian National Cycling Squad offered me a place on their team, I spoke no Farsi. My Iranian father had never taught us, and anyway he'd left the family not long after he taught me to ride my bike at age four.

The extent of my Farsi as a track sprinter for the Iranian team was '*Yek dor!*' meaning 'Last lap!' which the coach screamed at me from the middle of Tehran's velodrome. When I'd left track racing six months later, my language skills were little improved.

Now, with no command of Turkish, I played charades with the hardware shop assistant, and I must have been pretty good at it, because he eventually went back inside, then returned carrying a thin, wooden vegetable crate, metal wire, and pliers.

My attention turned to my purple aluminium bike, designed for urban activities like commuting to the office or grabbing a latte with friends, not for cycling the world. Lightweight and small-packing equipment was expensive, which meant mine was heavy and bulky and left serious questions about my ability to survive a winter. It also made my bicycle look ridiculously huge. My sleeping bag had cost me fifteen dollars and didn't even fit into my biggest pannier bag so was strapped on top of everything else behind my saddle. This bike was a world away from the expensive, lightweight carbon bikes I had ridden in sport.

Lucy and the shopkeeper watched as I removed the luggage hanging from the front wheel and tied it over the rear bags. I then knelt down and began attaching the vegetable crate to the front of the bike with wire. There was one rule about my bike that applied to everyone, including me: never touch it, because I never cleaned it. Within seconds, my hands were black and my face too, from wiping sweat from my brow.

Locals began gathering to watch the show, some blatantly hanging out of upper-storey windows. Word was spreading that the box was for the dog. My hands were bleeding from the wire, and the oil mixed in with the blood.

Once finished, I stood up and wiped my hands on my floral skirt, which was exactly why I had chosen such a pattern – to disguise the fact it was used as a tea towel for life. I touched the crate and it rocked from side to side. I looked underneath and noticed a thick piece of wood running down the centre of the crate's bottom. Bollocks. I hadn't noticed that before. Well, this was the best I could do with what I had. I cushioned the inside of the crate with clothing, making sure my red tartan Scottish cycling jersey was on top.

Sure, my dog carrier was wobbly, but still I was astounded I had achieved this engineering feat all by myself. I hadn't even worked out how to use a puncture repair kit. When I stood back looking at the bike, the box, and Lucy, however, I just shook my head. This was never going to work. But in the same moment, I thought: I have no choice; I have to make this work. And so I decided the best thing to do was ignore the fact it was impossible.

I wasn't ready to put Lucy in the box just yet, especially not in front of this crowd. Suddenly it became vital to buy her a water bowl. I knelt down, petting her head and explained I would be back in five minutes and she should wait with the bicycle. I hurried into the grocery store, not knowing if Lucy would wait. I found a silver tandoori bowl, way too heavy and too expensive, but I bought it, along with some cooked meat, and hurried out, worried she would be gone.

Seeing Lucy still sitting next to my bicycle flooded me with happiness. I placed the bowl of meat in front of her, but she was having none of it. I sighed and tipped the meat onto the pavement, where she gobbled it up. I kept my body close to hers, protecting her from the outside world of humans that frightened her so much.

I racked my brain for ways to prolong the impending moment of failure. Too many people had gathered, everyone wanting to see what happened when I tried to cycle with the big dog in the box. I couldn't believe I was about to do this. The only living things I had transported by bicycle were drunken friends after a night in the pub, which wasn't the best training, though at least it was a start.

I didn't want an audience when it all went wrong, especially in case I burst into tears. So I began walking the bike and Lucy along the street, away from the crowd. But watching Lucy limp, I knew we had no choice. Lucy had to go in the box. I had to push past my fear of failure and just do it.

I stopped and leaned the bike against a wall and squatted down to Lucy's level. I cupped her face gently in my hands and, looking in her eyes, explained softly. I didn't want to put her in the box and cycle her and she wouldn't want to either. But we had no choice. We had to do it. If we didn't, the dogs would attack her again. She wasn't safe. I explained that both of us would find the next 550 kilometres difficult and uncomfortable and perhaps at times even scary, but once she was at the sanctuary she would be protected for the rest of her life. Her big, chocolate-brown eyes looked back at me, and I hoped she somehow understood.

I scooped her up, repeating over and over what a good girl she was, and placed her in the box. Whispering for her to trust me, I stood back. She sat unmoving in the box, her eyes locked on mine. I held the bike steady and slowly pulled it away from the wall. I stalled, scared to do anything else, waiting for this moment to fall apart. I suddenly had the urge to burst out laughing, as I always did when I was nervous. Finally, I lifted one leg over the frame and stood for a moment, not quite believing Lucy hadn't jumped out yet.

People began to point and laugh. Lucy towered above the height of the handlebars. I took a deep breath and repeated what would be our mantra for the journey: 'You're a good girl, Lucy,' and we set off, weaving dangerously from side to side. Both Lucy's weight and the wobbly box were causing the front wheel to dip and swerve and I was sure I'd crash.

I was four years old when Dad called behind me, 'I've got you, I've got you – I'm holding on, I promise.' I glanced behind and saw that Dad wasn't hanging on at all. He was way behind in the distance. I was cycling all by myself. Suddenly overcome with fear, I wobbled and fell over.

Now, with Lucy, my heart raced, and it took all my strength to correct the weaving motion and keep the front wheel straight. We were moving. We were actually moving! Lucy kept glancing around to me and then back to the road, probably thinking she'd been rescued by a fruit loop. Everyone on the street stopped what they were doing and burst out laughing at the sight of a foreign girl cycling a bicycle overloaded with luggage and a big dog up front. I ignored them. I could take 550 kilometres of humiliation to ensure Lucy had a safe life.

A few minutes later, just as we had found some momentum, I realised I was desperate for the bathroom. I'd been so preoccupied with the box and Lucy that I hadn't noticed before, and I cursed myself for having gone through all that only to stop so soon.

I rode up to a petrol station and the staff turned to stare. I stopped and held the handlebars in place as I dismounted and lifted Lucy out of the box, giving her a big cuddle and setting her down on the ground. I explained to her that I was going to the toilet and would only be a minute. The staff must have thought I was nuts.

I went as fast as I could, but when I returned, Lucy wasn't there. I called her. Nothing. I scanned the surroundings. Nothing. I called again and again. Lucy was gone. I scolded myself for needing to pee. Eventually I gave up calling, and I pedalled reluctantly away. But then from a field opposite, Lucy came pounding towards me as fast as she could. The smile on my face and warmth in my heart were enormous as I set the bike down and waited with open arms. She reached me and I hugged her. 'I thought you were gone!' I said over and over.

She padded beside me as I pedalled slowly, and then once again I stopped and lifted her into the box and off we went. Cars passed close by, and it took my full concentration to stay in a straight line. A wobble could be fatal for both of us, and it reminded me of riding in the peloton.

Suddenly a van whizzed by, much too close, and shook the bike. Terror seized me. That was it. There was no way I could do this for 550 kilometres. It was simply too dangerous for both of us if I lost control. I had no choice. I was going to have to take her to a shelter here.

CHAPTER 3

I leant the bike against a bus stop in Biga's busy town centre. Predictably, people stopped to laugh at Lucy in the box, nudging their friends, so they too could laugh. I lifted Lucy down and stood on the busy pavement, asking strangers walking past where the local dog shelter was. No-one understood English. But I kept asking, over and over, all the while glancing back to make sure Lucy was still beside the bicycle.

Eventually a man stopped. He didn't understand me either, but he pulled out his phone and called a friend who spoke some English, enough for me to explain and get directions to the local dog shelter.

Grateful for the help, I pedalled on, ignoring my guilt by instead thinking about everyone around me who was *not* riding bicycles around the world, all of whom were in a better position to help this dog than I was.

I came to a junction where I was pretty sure I should turn to get to the shelter, but to be certain, I asked some men working on the roadside. One jumped out of his monster-sized yellow digger, and I pointed to different roads while repeating the words *köpek evi*, meaning 'dog house'. He pointed to the road I had suspected was correct, and then he walked beside me as I crossed the busy street. I was grateful, thinking it was a kind gesture on a dangerous stretch of road.

We had no sooner crossed the road when he reached over and stuck his hand down my shirt, grabbing my breasts. Shocked, I yanked his arm away and jumped back. For a second, we just looked at each other, and then I began shouting angrily at him. He appeared genuinely surprised at my reaction, with seemingly no idea what my anger was all about. Finally he shrugged and walked off, as though nothing had happened. I stood in disbelief. He had done this in daylight and in open sight of a busy road, making no attempt to hide his actions, which scared me a little. Perhaps this type of behaviour was considered acceptable in Turkey. I hoped not.

Suddenly, dogs began barking from an embankment above, and my anger turned to fear as I pedalled away as fast as I could, with Lucy running beside me. Arriving at the dog shelter, I was relieved to have escaped the awful man as well as the dogs, but still my guilt felt heavy at what I was about to do next. Cycling Lucy so far on busy roads was just too dangerous. I had tried, and I knew we wouldn't make it. This local shelter was our only option.

I left Lucy with the bicycle and went into a small office where two men were sitting. Right away I didn't like them and didn't trust them. Their eyes did not shine like those of good people. I used charades to explain I had a dog. They didn't seem to understand and so followed me outside, where I pointed to Lucy and then back to the shelter. They nodded their heads and motioned to bring her in. I went to Lucy and silently lifted her up. I couldn't speak to her. I had to cut off my emotions now.

Carrying her, I followed the men to an enclosure filled with barking dogs inside a dozen small cages. As I stood there, holding Lucy, a full-blown argument was escalating inside my mind:

Lucy will never get out of this cage, Ishbel!
That's the reality for street dogs in Turkey…
But she will die if you leave her!
No, you've done enough. This is not your country. You are cycling the
world. Put her in the cage and walk away.

I didn't like the men. I didn't like the cages. The animals didn't look happy. I looked into the eyes of one of the caged dogs, and suddenly I was certain. I turned with Lucy still in my arms and ran as fast as I could back to my bicycle. I heard the men's shouts, but I didn't stop. I didn't even put Lucy in the box. I cycled off with her running beside. I wanted to get away from that place as fast as possible. Away from that moment when I was going to leave Lucy alone in that horrible place with those horrible men.

Two months later, an animal rights video came out of that shelter showing a starving dog eating a dead puppy in his cage.

The village of my foster care placement was asleep and in darkness as the men drove me back. I wished I were asleep too and that this was a dream rather than a nightmare I couldn't wake up from. Earlier that night I had finished my Saturday shift stacking shelves and was walking back to my foster house. A dark blue car pulled over, and the men inside explained they were from Glasgow and had travelled up to camp by the loch but were lost. Even though the loch was only five minutes away, the men didn't understand my directions and asked me to show them, assuring me they'd bring me right back. They looked older, about 50 years or so, and so I trusted them, having been taught to be helpful and respect elders.

But they did not bring me straight back.

When they finally did, they turned onto the same road I walked each day for the school bus and stopped outside my foster house. That they knew where I lived swirled in my head, and yet I couldn't make sense of it. It would take me years to realise that they had lied when they told me they needed directions.

I opened the car door. They told me they would see me again. I just wanted to go home. That's all that I wanted. But I didn't have a real home anymore. I stepped out of the car and began walking up the steep driveway to my foster house. Suddenly, the driver got out and called me back. I turned back to him, petrified someone would hear. He wanted something else.

'Please no, I don't want to,' I pleaded in a whisper.

He was standing right in view of the house and I panicked that my foster carers would see him. I knew from when I was a little girl, some things you just kept a secret or it made things worse. I glanced back at my foster house and wanted so much to be inside, but I was here and the long driveway separated my two realities. I needed the men to go away before anyone saw.

'I really don't want to, please just go.'

'This is the last thing,' he promised, 'then we'll go.'

I walked back to him and knelt down. I went far away to a place with no feelings, but now I knew there was something I wanted even more now than going home. I wanted to die. Afterward, I slowly walked up the driveway in the darkness and pleaded with God to give me the strength to kill myself. To end this nightmare called life.

After fleeing the shelter, I knew there was simply no option but to cycle Lucy all the way to the sanctuary. I checked Google Maps and found an alternative route that was longer but on a small rural road, which would surely eliminate some of the traffic and reduce the danger.

To ride my bicycle on rough ground, however, had its own risks. Only days before, I had stood in a large garage surrounded by men in oil-stained overalls as I pointed to each of my repairs. A mechanic removed the sock that held my rear pannier rack onto the seat post, and the men, unable to contain themselves, doubled over into hysterical laughter. I laughed too – but not too hard.

My repairs may have seemed ridiculous to qualified mechanics, but using socks and zip ties had allowed me to pedal a thousand kilometres farther. Those repairs had kept me going on *tarmac*. Going off-road, well, my bike just might completely fall apart.

I took a few deep breaths. I suppose we'll soon see, I thought, and set off on the hardened dirt road with bushes and trees to each side and not much else.

I quickly realised that this was possibly the worst road I had ever cycled in my life, and I regretted my decision. The wheels slid this way and that on loose gravel and rocks as I weaved in between crater-sized pot-holes. Every second I thought I would crash, and it took all my strength not to. Losing control of the bike with Lucy in the box was not an option, and I knew I had to master riding this terrain quickly.

As I cycled on, I reminded myself that this road was mostly traffic-free and therefore safer. I practised on the rough terrain with Lucy walking beside. Before long I was riding without sliding all over the place, and so I lifted her back into the box.

We were just getting the hang of it as a team when greenery rustled in the distance, along the edge of the road. What was moving the bushes like that, I wondered. Then I heard barking – really angry barking. I couldn't see the dogs, but I knew they were there, and it sounded like a lot of them. I sped up, trying to put as much distance as possible between Lucy and me and the shaking bushes.

Glancing back, I saw a large pack of dogs tear out onto the road and charge toward us. Shit. Shit. Shit. They were angrier, fiercer, and wilder than any dogs I'd ever encountered. I remembered the dogs attacking Lucy in the village; these ones would rip her apart. They'd rip me apart.

Knowing that I couldn't ride fast enough to get away, I braked abruptly and Lucy jumped out. Throwing the bike down, I turned to face the charging animals. Survival instinct took over, which was a good thing considering I was scared of slugs, and before I realised what I was doing, I was shouting and charging toward the oncoming pack. If they got to Lucy, I couldn't save her. The dogs kept coming at us. What if they don't stop? I had a moment of doubt and fear. A picture of Lucy standing helpless beside the bike flashed through my mind, along with every life moment where I had stood alone and afraid, and I erupted into a force of power. Lucy was *not* going to die today.

I screamed that I would kill every single last one of them, and I absolutely believed it as I charged faster toward them. The lead dog hesitated and then stopped, and then they all stopped, standing in a group, still barking ferociously.

I kept pushing forward, stamping my feet and hollering. I was almost upon them. Oh God, this is going to hurt if I reach them. One dog turned away, a few followed, and then they were all running back the way they came. Still I kept charging forward, the adrenaline coursing through me, not yet realising it was over.

The world around me slowly came back into focus, and I dropped my arms to my sides and stopped moving. I stood in the middle of the road, my whole body shaking and tears streaming down my face.

I was in shock. At everything: the dogs, myself, my past. I felt awful about screaming I was going to kill them, and my fury shocked me. What had come over me? I hadn't even had a rabies vaccination, and one bite could be fatal. I knew if it were only myself I was protecting, I probably would have just stood and taken whatever was coming. Yet here I was risking my life to save this dog.

I knew I had to get her to safety. I turned and walked back to the bicycle, wiping away my tears with still-trembling hands. We had to keep moving.

Lucy had tried to squeeze herself under my bicycle for protection, but only half her body fit. As I got closer, I saw her wide eyes staring out from under the purple bicycle frame. I knew that look of fear well.

🚲

The old men came back for me, just as they had said they would. They called out from a parked car as I walked to my Saturday job at the shop. I turned and panicked. I noticed a new man in the back seat with a long, white, straggly beard. He was about 70 years old, and his eyes glistened with excitement. I felt sick. They told me to get in, that they had travelled a long way especially for me. I shook my head and began to back away. They laughed and said I had to get in because they had waited a long time for me. I surprised myself with how forceful my 'No!' was, and I ran as fast as I could.

I knew that all of this was my own fault because I was so bad, but still I was scared. Everyone was new in my life, and I didn't feel close enough to anyone to tell them about the men, certainly not my foster parents. Perhaps the men knew this, which made it a safer bet to target foster kids. I was so frightened. I knew they would come back for me again, and the next time I didn't think they would allow me to run so easily.

My foster carers were very supportive about me finishing school but had been honest about their motives to be foster carers. He had been a lawyer and she an accountant, and both had the idea to retire early with their two small children. They tried it, but within a year they'd realised the lifestyle they wanted cost more than they could afford. They saw an ad in the newspaper mentioning rates of pay for foster carers and applied. I don't know why it made a difference to me that they didn't look after me out of love. But it did. It made a big difference. I had been thrown from my own home because my mum didn't want me, and now I was with a new family who wanted me only for the money they got for looking after me. They ticked the boxes for their pay cheque, but with a lack of training and understanding, they were out of their depth, and although I knew they cared, I needed real love more than anything else in the world.

I lifted the bike off Lucy, and she went crazy, licking me all over. I knew I would protect her again and again, even if I risked my own life by doing so. On my own, I would have been debilitated by fear, but because I had Lucy to protect, adrenaline won out over fear, and I did what I needed to do to protect her.

After that, I was constantly scanning for the first signs of an attacking pack. And there were plenty of them across rural Turkey. Each time we encountered one, I'd stop, get off the bike and march toward the oncoming pack, waving my arms and shouting, 'I dare you, I dare you!' I figured out that there was one rule to keeping Lucy alive: I had to be alpha. I had to be alpha no matter how scary the danger we faced.

We cycled through village after village of crumbling buildings. I was hurting from the extra weight on the bicycle, and Lucy was hurting from the travelling. She refused to lie down in the box, preferring to sit up, looking out as we cycled. This was a worry because it gave me less warning if she was going to jump out, which was particularly nerve-wracking if a car or dogs approached.

Now that I had mastered the off-road conditions, we got into our routine. We would cycle a few kilometres with Lucy inside the box, and then she would get restless. At that point, I would set her down so that she could walk. She seemed to like the break from the box, but I noticed that her limping worsened if she walked too long, so I put her back in the box as soon as she'd sufficiently stretched her legs.

And so it went, mile after mile.

It was late afternoon when I arrived, exhausted, at the top of a tough climb and decided to take a break before cycling a little farther on to camp. I wanted to make sure we covered a good distance each day, but I also wanted to make sure it wasn't too tiring for Lucy, and so we stopped every few kilometres for rests.

I pushed my bike up a dirt track and found a small opening to a hidden field surrounded by hedgerows. The view was magnificent, and I leaned the bike against a tree and simply absorbed the scene. Sunshine bounced off the green valley below, which was dotted with lush meadows and farmland and surrounded by tree-covered hills. The only sign of human life was a tractor tending its field far off in the distance. I sighed contentedly; this was my reward for a hard day's cycling.

Then, out of the blue, my tyre punctured all by itself as the bike lay still against the tree. Bollocks! I'm not bloody fixing that now. Lucy had already given up on the day and was fast asleep by my bike. I was exhausted myself. I looked around at the vast, empty expanse around me and thought, sod it, I'll just camp here.

That decided, I sat down to enjoy my very own widescreen cinema, with nature the starring diva. Lucy woke up and wandered over to me. She flopped down half on my lap and half on the ground and dozed off again. Stroking her head as she slept, I marvelled at the connection between us. I wasn't even a dog person, to be frank. When I'd moved into my ex-boyfriend's home, I had been very clear that the Labrador he shared with his ex-wife could stay only one night a week. When he asked me why, I shrugged, explaining I didn't want to share my house with a dog because I'd feel unclean and would have to wash my hands all the time because of all the grime. Just then Lucy's paw came up to scratch her ear vigorously, and I laughed about how content I was now to share my lap with a flea-ridden dog. I pulled her in tight and thought, I love you.

I cooked dinner, sharing half with Lucy. She was so hungry, she finally ate straight from the bowl rather than from the ground or a rubbish bag. I quietly celebrated this victory.

As darkness approached, I pitched the tent, and then we sat watching the sky change to a brilliant pink over the valley as the sun went down. I usually felt anxious when wild camping, but tonight, with Lucy beside me, I felt no fear and I noticed what a pleasant change it was to enjoy my night-time surroundings in peace.

I said goodnight to Lucy, giving her a hug. She still refused to sleep inside the tent with me and went to her place outside at the foot of the tent.

CHAPTER 4

My eyes shot open in the darkness. I didn't dare even the motion of a breath. Lying still in my sleeping bag, I concentrated hard, using only sound to visualise the scene outside. Male voices, loud and drunken, not far from my tent. The ruttering of an engine, perhaps from a tractor. I was well hidden, camped in a secluded spot surrounded by hedgerows, trees, and empty fields as far as the eye could see. No-one knew I was here.

The men began shouting. Holy shit. They got louder. I squeezed my eyes tight and pretended this wasn't happening. There's no way they were shouting at me. But who else could they be shouting at? I tried to count the number of voices, but there were too many and I realised in that moment, whatever was going to happen was probably out of my control. I lay still and hoped it would all just go away. Did they want to do me harm?

I knew what it felt like when men wanted to hurt me. I knew the feeling of watching a fist come toward my face, unable to do anything because I'm held down by my neck. Of that millisecond when I can't see the fist anymore. Then the crushing impact on my nose. Of being rolled up in a carpet, having no idea what's coming next, and then being stamped on as my mind goes to a place far away. Of using all my force to fight back, but running out of energy and eventually knowing it's best not to fight back. Even Lucy understood that.

Oh God, they're definitely shouting at me, I thought with a start, as my mind jerked back to the situation I was currently in. Panic stricken, I lay there, frozen. Then I thought of Lucy. She was outside. I couldn't hear her. Was she in danger? Dogs seemed to be hated in Turkey, or at least in the parts I'd seen. What would they do to her? I wished with all my heart Lucy was inside with me. Because then I could curl up in a ball in the middle of my tent and pretend this wasn't happening. But Lucy was outside and I had to make sure she was OK.

I slowly pulled on the entrance zipper, and each time it made a noise I froze, my face screwing up in horror. I paused, not daring to look out or draw attention to myself. But I had to for Lucy. I peeked out and saw a tractor, with its engine running and lights illuminating the surrounding area. Several men stood jostling around on the trailer behind it, raising beer cans in the air and shouting toward my tent. Shit.

I couldn't see Lucy. And these men were not going away. I had to do something to change my reality. Remembering that snarling pack of attacking dogs, I shouted as forcefully and alpha as I could: 'Go away!'

A voice shouted back in thickly accented English, 'Do you want me? Do you want me?' and the others burst out laughing. They began jumping over the side of the trailer and crossing into the field toward my tent. Holy crap. This was not the change I wanted. I hoped Lucy had run away and was safe, and I began begging to no-one in particular, don't let this be happening, please don't let this be happening.

A deep growling filled the air. The men froze and became silent. The growling grew louder and louder and terrified even me. Lucy's shape appeared in the darkness, moving slowly toward the men. Oh God, Lucy, please don't do that.

She stopped between the men and my tent. I got ready because if any one of them got to her, I would attack them with everything I had. Lucy lowered her front legs and head as though she was preparing to pounce and, remaining in that position, growled menacingly. The men turned and ran as fast as they could shouting, '*Köpek! Köpek!*', 'Dog! Dog!', jumping back in their trailer as the engine powered up and rumbled them off into the darkness.

Lucy remained in position, with her ears and nose to the air, and I remained still, not making a sound. Finally, she turned around and padded back to me. Bowing her head, she licked my hand. I hugged her with everything I had, whispering, 'Thank you,' over and over. This street dog had done something no human ever had. She had rescued me.

I invited Lucy inside the tent, but she refused and went back to her spot outside. I wondered if she was guarding me as I slept. I got back into my sleeping bag but was unable to sleep. If this had happened just two days before, there would have been no Lucy protecting me. I thought back to our first meeting, with me cycling away and Lucy chasing me as hard as she could, and I wondered, who was rescuing whom?

When I was 16 years old and in foster care, I was desperate to be rescued. The day I ran away from the men, I called Mum from the village phone box and pleaded with her to let me come home. I said I would be good. Said I would do everything she asked me to do, without questioning. I would be the girl she wanted me to be. I knew I would because I knew the alternative if I didn't. But she refused. I broke down sobbing, begging her now to give me one more chance. I would be good. I promised I would be good. But she said no. She said I had to change. That if I didn't change, bad things would happen. Desperate, I told her the truth I hadn't wanted to say, that bad things had already happened, that men had made me do things, awful things. There was a pause, and then she told me that I had to change or these things would keep happening to me. It seemed to me that her voice had no compassion, no care at all. That was the moment I knew I was never going home, and something inside me broke.

After that phone call to Mum, I spent more time contemplating suicide than I did doing my homework. I sat in my foster house bedroom for hours, staring at the blade, hating myself. *You are such a horrible girl even your own family don't like you.* I pressed the blade against my wrist. I knew I had to do it vertically, to make sure. One small cut would end it all. I wouldn't be in this hell anymore. Pressing harder into the skin, I willed myself to do it. Just do it. Just do it. But I was pathetic and didn't have the guts to do it, and I hated myself even more.

Not being dead meant I had to deal with the old men, and I did this by running away from foster care. Still clinging to dreams of university, even though that future was slipping away, I ran no farther than the town that my school was in, some 20 miles away.

But all I did was run into a new hell.

CHAPTER 5

I awoke early the next morning. After the previous night's encounter, I was eager to make this place a distant memory.

I began my usual morning routine of packing up, playing with Lucy in between tasks. Everything seemed better with her around. I was pulling tent pegs out of the ground when a big, blue tractor drove into the field and stopped. I watched a man climb out and limp toward me. I tried to assess if he was happy, angry or indifferent, but he was too far away to tell.

It took him quite some time to reach me, and when he did, I saw he was so old, he had shrunk. He said nothing, but rather broke out into a gummy smile that swallowed up his dark leathery face and wrinkles. I said hello. He just continued smiling. We stood like that for a few moments, until finally I politely excused myself, explaining I was packing up to leave as I had a lot of kilometres to cycle. I don't know why I said anything; he couldn't understand me.

I bent over to remove another tent peg from the ground and suddenly, with ninja speed, he began slapping my behind with the palm of his hand. I jumped up in shock. He was still wearing that gummy smile, his eyes twinkling like crazy. I wanted to puke. And I was flooded with rage. Perhaps if last night hadn't happened, I would have been more mindful of his age, but I screamed at him wildly that he was a disgusting old man and that Allah was looking down on him.

With a look of shock and fear, he turned and tried to hustle back to his tractor, but he was so old, he could only limp. It was the slowest getaway I had ever seen. I almost cheered him on as he finally reached his tractor and drove away. Lucy lay in the grass watching us without moving, perhaps sensing I didn't need rescuing on this occasion.

I finished breaking down the tent and took a last look around me. Mist rose up from the surrounding hills, and I sucked in the coolness of the early morning air, pushing away negative thoughts of last night's and this morning's encounters, instead enjoying the serenity before the hardship of riding this rough road again. Cycling off-road on an aluminium city bike designed for tarmac, with no suspension, thin tyres, little tread and overloaded with luggage, plus a 20-kilo dog in a vegetable crate over the front wheel, made progress painfully slow.

I wasn't on the bike long that morning before I was burning up. It may have been winter in Turkey, but it was still warmer than Scotland's hottest day of summer. This was the toughest cycling experience of my whole life, and we still had 530 kilometres to go. Each time I came to a steep hill, which was every few turns of the twisting track, my handlebars went this way and that over the unpredictable gravel and stones. Weighted down with Lucy and so much luggage, I couldn't cycle fast enough to use forward motion to cruise over the uneven ground and short, sharp hills. To make it easier, Lucy walked the steepest uphills.

I finally arrived, red-faced, at a small village after a long, dusty climb. Stopping to catch my breath, I spotted a group of shepherds with their animals ahead. Despite the searing heat, I pulled on a merino wool sweater over my vest top. Discouraging their attention seemed more important than risking death from self-combustion. Regardless of beliefs about freedom of choice, as a solo female exploring foreign lands, life was just easier if I dressed for social expectations as well as climatic conditions.

In Iran, where I had cycled for the national team, women are not allowed to do many things because of their gender. We are not allowed to sing, dance, or show our hair in public. Women, including a few of my teammates, had even been arrested for cycling. Turkey surprised me. I had assumed that because there was no law enforcing hijab, women wouldn't wear it. But every woman I passed in rural Turkey wore hijab, and it reminded me of my dad and Iran.

My life on two wheels began when I was still in nappies, and I suppose I had an Islamic revolution to thank for that. In 1979, the year before I was born in England, the Iranian Revolution took place nearly 4,000 miles away. Much to the horror of those who voted for change, their new leader, Ruhollah Khomeini, known in the West as Ayatollah Khomeini, declared Iran an Islamic republic and his interpretation of Islam now controlled all aspects of human life, with the new laws brutally enforced. I was still in Mum's womb, with her due date nearing, when Khomeini declared that all Iranians living throughout the world should return home to Iran. To encourage compliance, money leaving Iran was blocked; the payments sent each month by Dad's well-off family to support him as a student and soon-to-be father ceased. Overnight my family was thrust into a life of extreme poverty.

The bicycle became an important and valuable tool for our survival. As a baby, I was strapped into a seat on the back of my father's bicycle as he pedalled through thick city traffic to buy potatoes that were a few pennies cheaper on the other side of the city. A heavy sack of spuds was then tied behind me on the bicycle, and we cycled home through the congestion and fumes.

Dad finished his studies full of hope, but jobless. Britain was a highly racist country in 1980; being in a mixed-race marriage was considered shameful, and my family was shunned. After the American Embassy siege in Tehran began in 1979, when 52 American diplomatic staff were taken hostage and held for 444 days, the hatred toward Iranians exploded. No-one wanted to employ an Iranian. I was two years old when my family had no choice but to move from England to Scotland so that Dad could work for his father-in-law as a roofer in the family business. The tiny village where we moved to was surrounded by farmland and had a big country park nearby. Sitting on the back of Dad's bike as he pedalled on his days off in fresh air was so much better than in the city smog we'd left behind.

🚲

I took a deep breath in and held it as I passed through the herd of goats, cows and shepherds, and hoped Lucy knew to hold her breath too. Past the herd, I noticed a teahouse on my left filled with black moustaches. The men stopped drinking and turned to stare at me in silence. Feeling self-conscious, I kept my gaze ahead and followed the road around the village, cycling back through the same group of shepherds and once more arriving at the teahouse. My face reddened with embarrassment as I wondered how it was possible to miss my exit out of a one-street village. The men were staring once more, probably wondering who was this girl riding in circles around their village. She couldn't possibly be lost, so what was she doing?

But I was lost. In this tiny, one-street village.

The sun was sweltering, and I decided tea was a magnificent idea – and perhaps there was a chance of breakfast. I came to a stop directly outside the open teahouse. '*Lütfen,*' I said, meaning 'Please,' and pointed to the big, silver tea dispenser. A man walked over, smiling politely, and

handed me a glass of hot Turkish tea. I didn't feel comfortable going inside with all those moustaches, so I stood sipping, with the bicycle still between my legs, ready to cycle if there was any trouble.

I concentrated on each sip of tea, with 20 men watching and Lucy lying in the sun a few metres away, her eyes trained on me. At that time, I did not know that local women were not allowed into teahouses in rural Turkey. If I had known, I would have gone in and sat down. I had been told too many times in Iran that I was 'not allowed' because I was a woman.

I remembered when the Iranian police had tried to stop me riding my bike. I decided on the spot that I would go to prison because no man was going to tell me not to ride my bike. I shouted back, telling them to move out of my way. They shouted at me and I at them. They shouted louder, and I screamed at the top of my lungs, 'I'm riding my bike!' There was a tense silence. It was clear that one of two things was about to happen: either I would be arrested or I would cycle away. The guards hesitated because I was shouting in English, and being a foreigner offered me some protection. A girl on a bike was not worth the international backlash that would come in the media. And so I pedalled on.

A man from the teahouse walked over and began speaking to me, but I had no idea what he was saying. He passed to the side of the teahouse and stood in front of a set of tall, green metal doors. Opening the doors slightly, he beckoned for me to follow him. Aye, right! I'm not going anywhere. I shook my head and stood where I was. He disappeared inside and reappeared a few moments later, beckoning me once more to come in. I pretended I didn't understand what he meant. The man opened the door further and I glimpsed a woman standing in a yard, her eyes darting about, like she didn't want to be seen. Her eyes met mine and she smiled. She opened her arms wide, beckoning me in.

CHAPTER 6

The woman's smile was warm, and I trusted her immediately. Lucy padded behind as I wheeled my bicycle through the big, green doors into the dusty yard of a house, with small huts for animals and fields behind as far as the eye could see. Chickens ran about, and I glanced at Lucy, knowing this could be disastrous. To my relief, she took no notice.

The woman and I stood facing each other in the yard, she with her hijab, I with my bicycle. She looked me up and down with what was clearly pity. I glanced self-consciously down to see the holes all over my clothes, and then looked back at her and saw she was smiling. She reached out and gently pulled a leaf and twig from my hair. I was surprised they were in there, but then again, I couldn't remember when I last brushed my hair. I didn't even own a hairbrush.

The woman was dressed in typical clothes for rural Turkey – a mustard wool cardigan over a long wool sweater and a long, loose skirt. Her hair was covered by a scarf. She pointed to herself and said 'Aysun,' and I pointed to myself and said 'Ishbel.' She motioned for me to follow her up the steep steps into the house. I nodded and followed her in, leaving Lucy with the job of protecting my bicycle, which she had begun to take very seriously, never straying far away.

Aysun led me into a bedroom with modern fitted wardrobes and a mirrored dresser, all of which seemed far removed from the crumbling village just outside. She pulled out different items of clothing and piled the bundle on the bed: a huge pair of traditional Turkish trousers, black with bright pink flowers; a long tunic sweater; a thick wool cardigan; a white vest; and a huge pair of white pants. I smiled, but inside I was horrified. These clothes were for winter in Russia, not sweltering Turkey.

Gesturing to a hairbrush on the dresser, Aysun took me to a shower room and handed me some toiletries. I got very excited about the soap and shampoo. My last real shower had been some 300 kilometres ago in Istanbul, although I did use wet wipes daily to clean up.

The shower was hot and soothing. I savoured each moment while also trying to wash as fast as I could, not wanting to use up all the solar-heated water. I turned off the shower, and before I had even stepped out of the stall, a knock came on the bathroom door. I froze for a moment, a little fearful, but then pulled a towel around me and opened the door.

Aysun stood there, motioning me to follow her back to the bedroom, where she left me alone again to get dressed. I put the white pants on and they went right up to my chest. If I had stretched them, they would have covered my head, too. I was giggling so much I had to cover my mouth with my hand to be quiet. I pulled on the vest, trousers and top, leaving the stifling sweater on the bed. Looking in the mirror, I saw a Turkish mountain granny gazing back at me and broke out laughing.

The feel of clean clothes against my skin was wonderful. I reached for the hairbrush and tried to brush my hair but soon gave up. Instead, I sat on the bed untangling the knots with my fingers and feeling a bit overwhelmed at the kindness of complete strangers. I thought of going into foster care and how not one family member had ever visited me. I'd asked why and had been told it was because I was in a village so far away, an answer I accepted without question. But now, cycling the world, I realised that 40 miles wasn't a lot of distance between family.

In the kitchen, Aysun was busy cooking eggs, and a spread of bread, cheese, jam, olives and tea was laid on the table. She motioned for me to sit and then served me the eggs. I didn't want to be rude, but I knew I couldn't sit and eat breakfast knowing that Lucy hadn't eaten yet. I gestured toward the door, scooped up half my eggs, a bit of cheese, and some bread into a napkin, and excused myself. Once Lucy was lying in the sun with a full belly, I happily returned to demolish the traditional Turkish breakfast.

Afterwards, we sat together on a big, blue sofa in the living room, surrounded by photos of Aysun's family on the walls. The respect and appreciation in both of our eyes diminished any awkwardness from the language barrier, and we used charades to communicate. She imitated working in the fields and that she began when the sun rose and stopped when the sun fell. She proceeded to show me her pains from the work. Her hands were red and sore, and she pulled up her sweater to expose her back, which she indicated caused her the worst pain.

I am qualified in holistic therapies and could see the muscular tension across her back. Motioning her to sit down, I gently massaged the solid muscles. Aysun was very thankful and hugged me tightly when I finished.

She then proudly showed me photos of her children at university. I saw her eyes change and in that moment, I understood. It had all been for her children. She suffered all that pain, working in the fields, to give her children the opportunity of a better life.

I thought of Mum and how she had struggled financially to look after us because Dad disappeared and never gave her any money. Even so, I received my first 'big girl' bike when I was seven years old. Mum had saved hard so I could have it. It was pink with a white basket on the front, where my teddy bear sat.

I rode that bicycle a lot. But not because I enjoyed cycling; actually I wanted a horse so badly, my bike became my horse. 'Giddy-up!' I'd call as I pedalled around the declared boundaries of the housing development streets that my freedom extended to. I had to cycle as fast as I could to make it more believable that I was riding a horse – because horses were fast. Sometimes I would slow down to allow my horse to trot and to catch my breath, but mostly I loved to feel the air on my face and my waist-length brown hair flying behind me.

Growing up meant that the time had arrived when my imagination was no longer strong enough for me to believe I was riding a horse, and I lost interest in cycling. My 'horse' was retired to the shed. I wouldn't have believed you then if you had told me I'd be riding a bicycle around the world and that instead of a teddy bear I'd have a dog in a basket on the front of my bike.

I explained to Aysun that I had to be setting off because I had many kilometres to cycle before it got dark. She disappeared and returned with bundles of cheese and bread. I thanked her and motioned I would change out of her clothes, but she stopped me, insisting I wear them. I shook my head vigorously, but Aysun disappeared again and returned with the wool sweater. *Oh no, not the wool sweater!*

She stood back, waiting for me to put it on. I tried to explain that I was Scottish and didn't need to wear a wool sweater in Turkey's heat. She understood nothing and stood smiling and waiting. I sighed and pulled on the sweater. Then she produced a scarf and without asking tied it over my head as a hijab. I didn't think anyone had ever looked at me with such happiness as she did in that moment. I glanced in the mirror at Muslim Mountain Granny and wondered how life had got to this point.

Lucy gave me a funny look when I grabbed the bike as if thinking *wow, what happened to you?* Aysun led me to the gates and then stood to the side, indicating that she wasn't allowed to be seen by the men in the teahouse. This saddened me. She seemed a prisoner in her own life, but I took some comfort that she lived in this nice house and not others I had seen.

We said goodbye and I returned to the street in front of the teahouse, where the men still sat. Aysun's husband came over, beaming with joy and pride and making grand gestures about the improvement in my appearance. I thanked him and cycled off, with Lucy trotting beside. There was no way I was putting Lucy in the box in front of all the watching men in the teahouse. And anyway, I had to find my way out of the village as fast as possible to get all those warm clothes off.

Minutes later, as I was preparing to pull the sweater off, two kids appeared beside me, riding an old motorbike and cheering me on with happy smiles and no helmets. I smiled back, sweating profusely, knowing self-combustion was imminent. After what seemed like an eternity, they waved goodbye and turned back for their village. I immediately braked and when I was sure they had disappeared, I ripped off the sweltering clothes.

I cycled on, thinking about the woman working in the fields all day with her sore back for the sake of her children.

The first time Dad left, I was four years old. He snuck out in the middle of the night, leaving a note to explain he was too disgusted with Mum to say goodbye to her face. At the time, Mum was pregnant with my brother Rory. She didn't know what she had done, but Dad had got angry when she changed the television channel without asking. Dad got disgusted at Mum a lot, sometimes not speaking to her for weeks at a time.

A month before Rory was born, Mum told Dad if he didn't come home now, he'd never be allowed back. So Dad came home.

But a few months later he left again. Even though his bag was packed at home, none of us believed he was actually leaving. We were in the park having a picnic, playing games, laughing and feeding the ducks. We were having such a good time we all thought Dad must have changed his mind. That he wasn't leaving us. That we were good enough for him to stay. But when we got home, Dad picked up his bag and said goodbye.

His progress to the door was slow because my brother Gavin was hanging onto his leg, screaming, 'Don't go, Daddy, please don't go.' I glanced up, and then continued my drawing. I held my breath, bit my lip and concentrated hard on drawing a horse. All of a sudden it became the most important thing in the world not to cry.

椖

I was only a few kilometres on from Aysun and the teahouse village when, out of nowhere, I punctured.

Bollocks. This was very unfortunate. I had cycled hundreds of kilometres, and across 13 countries at this point in my life, yet I had never actually *fixed* a puncture. I had only replaced punctured tubes with new ones. But I had no tubes left.

It didn't usually bother me that I didn't know how to fix a puncture, as there was always someone around happy to do it. But in Turkey, I had not seen women riding bicycles and I really didn't want to ask a man to fix my puncture because my experience had so far taught me that he would likely ask for something unwanted and inappropriate in return. This was motivation enough to finally learn how to fix a puncture myself, and I pulled into a field with some stone ruins that I could lean my bike against.

It took me a long time to find the hole without a bucket of water, but I finally did, and I celebrated with a little victory dance. Then I had to find the hole again. I put the repaired tube back in the tyre, and then Lucy and I ate some bread with cheese before setting off again.

I turned out of the field, and within seconds, the front wheel punctured again. I sighed heavily and fixed the puncture at the side of the road, and set off again. And again, it punctured. Now I was raging. I'd had enough of fixing punctures and decided the best plan of action was to keep stopping to pump up my tyre until I got to the next town to buy tubes.

By late that afternoon, the sun was scorching. I stood with my mouth open wide to the sky and squeezed my empty water bottle above me. The last drop of water had passed some moments before. But still I stood in that position, hoping for just one more sip. I was struggling with the heat, weight, dust, pot-holes, gravel, punctures and hills. I was so thirsty, my throat hurt.

A white car passed slowly and then stopped ahead of me. A man got out and I was immediately wary. He was short, round, bald and in his fifties. His shirt was open at the neck and tucked into grey trousers ending in dusty black shoes. He smiled. I hesitated, and then asked for *su,* meaning 'water'. He nodded and reached into his car. He pulled out a bottle of water with a big smile. Standing where he was, he held out the bottle toward me. I leaned in closer, reaching for it, but then he pulled it back. I looked at him confused, and he began shaking the bottle, cheerily singing, 'Sex – sex – sex.' Disgusted and angry, I pressed my foot on the pedal to cycle away. The man looked confused, and he pointed at me and him, again repeating his song. I shook my head vigorously and began cycling away with Lucy trotting at my side.

I heard the car engine start up behind me and suddenly felt vulnerable, conscious of how narrow this road was, with nowhere to hide. Oh God, please don't run me over, I prayed, as the car approached from behind. I held my breath, every muscle tense, and as the car passed, I breathed out again.

Cycling around the very next corner, I saw water running out of a pipe in a stone wall on the side of the road. I dropped my bike and ran toward it, collapsing to my knees and using my hands to scoop water into my mouth, not giving a damn if the water was fit for human consumption. I filled up all my water bottles, including the two-litre one I used for my shower, because now I had Lucy and I didn't allow her to drink from the muddy puddles like she wanted.

Refreshed, we were back on the road. Although my skills had improved with practice, it still took tremendous concentration to cycle with Lucy in the box over my front wheel. Every moment of pedalling, I was watching three things: Lucy, the road and the surrounding area. I used my voice soothingly to relax and also control Lucy, as she was in no way restrained in the box. Sometimes she would start to stand up, and I had to quickly slow down with no jerking movement and settle her back down. Most of the time I was cycling with one hand while using the other to pet Lucy. At the same time, I watched the road in front of my wheel because pot-holes, bumps, gravel and rocks are perilous for any cyclist on a road bike. I watched the surrounding area to spot when greenery moved in order to give me a few extra seconds to brake and set Lucy and the bike down, ready to take on the dog packs. Dogs are territorial, and I was cycling an injured dog through their land.

I arrived at a junction with one of the most beautiful sights I could possibly see at that moment: a smooth tarmac road! It looked wonderful, and I imagined riding it and not bumping up and down. Smooth tarmac meant I wouldn't have to concentrate so much on the road, which would give my mind as well as my muscles a rest.

A giant billboard loomed at the start of the junction. This would make a perfect spot to camp, as the sign would hide me from the road. After last night, I wasn't taking chances on my tent being seen. I decided my ride on the smooth tarmac could wait for tomorrow. I was exhausted, not only from the cycling but because of a sleepless night.

I set up my tent and then immediately lay down in it, with the entrance open and one arm stretched outside to pet Lucy, who was lying in the tent's small porch. As the sun went down, I watched her and wondered what horrors she had been through. What caused her to walk so strangely? Her deformed paw looked as though it had been rolled over and flattened. But the limp seemed to come from her hip. When I got her to the sanctuary, I would ask that she have a thorough checking-over from a vet.

She was so thin and so scared of the world around her. I questioned if her tail worked at all; it was always tucked down inside her back legs. I wondered if she had been on her own when she had endured such pain. I hoped she hadn't been all alone. But it was clear that she had suffered; after all, she was a street dog, and from what I'd seen in Turkey so far, it was a street dog's lot to suffer, alive or in death.

That night, she again refused to come inside my tent, instead staying outside, guarding me. During the night, however, she tried to push her nose through my tent door at least three times. But when I opened the flap, she only peeked in, gave me a kiss and then disappeared to guard duty again.

CHAPTER 7

I woke up happy, knowing I would see Lucy, and eagerly unzipped the tent. She was waiting, her tail doing helicopters. So the tail worked after all! She stuck her head inside my tent for morning cuddles. I was smitten, and so glad to have her with me. All this travelling wasn't good for Lucy, and cycling with her on my bike was certainly hard on me, but I knew it was worth it to get her off the streets. I understood the reality of a life without safety, in a world where predators exist in invisible corners, waiting for easy prey.

I climbed out of the tent to brew my coffee, and when I turned back to the tent, I was delighted to see Lucy inside, fast asleep. My joy lasted just a moment, though, before it turned to horror as I remembered her fleas. My instinct was to move her as fast as possible.

I rushed toward the tent's entrance, then stopped. She looked so comfortable, and it wasn't her fault she was covered in fleas, plus it was a huge step forward that she was inside the tent. So rather than moving her, I sat back down and decided to be OK with sharing her fleas, making a mental note to find flea treatment in the next town.

I let her sleep for a bit, but because I was eager to begin our day I soon packed us up and set off onto the heaven of smooth tarmac. Both my body and mind soaked up the blessed absence of bumpy off-road discomforts. Whenever I heard trucks, I would stop pedalling and lean over the handlebars to hold Lucy in my arms. She was never scared when she was in my arms. I loved making her feel safe.

⚲

When I was seven years old, I visited Dad at his home in England. My brothers and I were all in a room, playing with toys on the floor. A friend of Dad's was there, and he asked me to sit on his knee. When I did, his hand travelled up the inside of my leg. That was the moment when I knew, really knew deep down, that I was a bad and awful girl. And I began hating myself. Just like that.

By the time I was nine, I was punishing myself for being bad by not eating. At 11, I wanted to die. By 13, I was consumed by self-hatred and thought of ways to kill myself. Still, I tried to be good, to please Mum. But at 14, something changed inside me, and questioning became more important to me than being a good girl. Mum responded in anger, trying to regain control, which seemed essential to her being able to cope.

I was miserable at home, but school was a different story. I was a straight-A student, winning awards each year for outstanding achievements, with my grades placing me in the top five per cent of British students. Academically there was nothing I couldn't achieve, and I felt destined for great things. Despite everything going on at home, I worked hard at school with a goal to study hard and get a degree and a good job. School was my hope and my escape.

⚲

After a few kilometres of pedalling, I rode into the rush-hour traffic of a busy town and had to concentrate hard to avoid car doors opening and people with their eyes on their mobile phones stepping out blindly onto the road. As usual, people pointed at me and laughed and I felt embarrassment, which then turned to anger. Lucy is in this box on my bicycle because the animals in your country suffer so badly, I thought. I told Lucy she was a good girl and to ignore them. Telling her this helped me ignore them too.

I knew I had a left turn coming up and stopped to check Google Maps on my phone. Normally I referred to maps only in very large cities, because I found it annoying and difficult if I missed an exit in seven lanes of traffic. Otherwise, I barely used maps.

The first time I went cycle touring outside my own country was to the Pyrenees in France, and I was on my own because my best friend had to cancel at the last minute. She had been the one with all the common sense for the trip, which included knowing how to read a map. I started out trying to use her maps but found that I spent all day of every day lost. So I threw the maps away and was never lost again. My navigating goals changed, and I pedalled in the general direction of another country or ocean with everything in between a surprise. This suited my personality and skills much better. But here, with Lucy, time was an important factor, and following the map would hopefully make us more efficient.

I turned left and faced a massive climb. Usually on steep hills I would let Lucy out of the box in order to lighten the load, but this time I kept her in the box because the road was so busy, and on the tarmac I could ride faster than she could walk.

The climb hurt more than expected, but to avoid thinking about the pain, I focused on the flea treatment I would buy for Lucy. Finally, on a long, empty stretch of road, I spotted a shop standing on its own. I pulled up just outside the door and stopped.

I leaned the bike against the wall next to the entrance and knelt down to Lucy. When I left her outside shops in order to go indoors to the bathroom or to buy food, she wouldn't be there when I returned, which confused me as I knew how seriously she took her task of guarding my bike. Instead, she would run to one of the surrounding fields to hide and watch for my return, and then she would run as fast as she could to join me as I pedalled away. At first this caused me some anxiety, until I realised that she was always watching from somewhere and would join me again. However, I wanted her to feel safe, so this time I spent some moments reassuring her and telling her she was OK and that she didn't need to run away anymore because she was safe and with me.

Satisfied that we had an understanding, I entered the shop and picked up tins of tuna for Lucy and bread for me. I paid and exited the shop only to see the owner flapping his arms to chase Lucy away. Lucy was half running away, half looking back at the shop entrance. I hollered 'Oy! That's my dog!' and took a few enraged steps toward the man, using the same wild arm movements he had used with Lucy. He stopped waving and looked genuinely petrified, so I dropped my arms and returned to my bicycle. Lucy kept her distance.

I cycled slowly off, and Lucy began running toward me, as usual. As she reached me, I got off the bike and held her in my arms at the side of the road. I felt terrible that she had been deliberately frightened and chased away after I had told her that she was safe and that she could trust me. Why were people so horrible to dogs? I didn't understand. I dug out the one pretty thing I had, a pastel neck scarf that I loved dearly, and tied it around her neck gently. I hoped this would be a sign and a warning to people that this dog had a human.

I was heading south through the Çanakkale region when I cycled into the town of Yenice, 150 kilometres from the western coast of Turkey, and pulled into a petrol station to charge my phone. Men dressed in hunting gear with rifles beside them sat eating breakfast at a red plastic table outside the café. One spoke a little bit of English, and he introduced the whole group to me, cheerfully explaining that they were going hunting. I didn't like hunting, and so immediately, I didn't like these men.

He asked what I was doing, and I explained that I was from Scotland and was cycling the world. No-one ever believed me when I said this. I was a 37-year-old woman on my own, and for some reason this was just too ridiculous to imagine. People always asked me where my husband and children were, and my answer – that I had neither – caused great shock.

They invited me to sit down. I didn't like the thought of sitting down with them, but there was nowhere else to sit where I could watch my phone charging. I called Lucy over, but she wasn't going near any shop entrance and instead remained by my bicycle, watching me.

The men finished eating, and I asked if I could feed my dog their leftovers. I patted my knees and called Lucy over. The men looked concerned seeing her limp and her deformed paw. I explained our story, which the one man translated back to his friends. They asked me if I wanted them to shoot her. I declined politely, telling them if they shot Lucy, I would kill each one of them with my bare hands. Everyone laughed, apart from me. When they saw I wasn't laughing, they explained they liked dogs and had only offered to shoot her in order to save her suffering.

A small police van pulled into the petrol station. It was the first opportunity I had seen for a lift that would not include the driver asking for something in return. Even 15 kilometres would be welcome. I walked over and asked if he would drive Lucy and me to the next town. I must have been desperate because when he said no, I turned away and immediately burst out crying. The hunters asked why I was upset, and I explained that men kept stopping and asking me for sex and that dogs attacked Lucy. The hunters motioned for me to sit back down and said that they would help. After making a few phone calls, they found out that one of their friends was driving a truck and would be passing a point about 30 kilometres away in a short time. They walked over to an old rusty car, speaking to one another in Turkish. Opening the boot, the English-speaking man told me to get my bicycle.

'There's no way my bike is going to fit in there,' I exclaimed.

'Yes, it will,' he assured me, and the others nodded vigorously, smiling. 'You are getting that truck. He is our friend and there will be no harm to you.'

I dismantled my bicycle and gear, and they tried to get it all inside their car. It seemed utterly impossible that it was going to fit, but their positive attitudes and repeated attempts had me doubled over in laughter. Defeat was not in their vocabulary, and when the boot finally closed with bike and gear inside, we all cheered and clapped.

There was really only enough space for the driver, Lucy, and me, but another of the hunters managed to squeeze in, too. We said our goodbyes and set off. I didn't think we had nearly enough time to reach the truck, but the men kept saying we'd make it, and I found myself a passenger in a terrifying Formula One race through the narrow twisting tracks of rural Turkey. And then suddenly, there was a truck, parked on the side of the road in the middle of nowhere. How had the truck driver even known where to stop?

The driver was standing in the back of the truck. We all got out of the rusty car, and the men pulled my belongings out and lifted them up above our heads to the truck driver. Then they wanted to lift Lucy up and over, too. Shit. The storage area was made of wooden slats and had gaping spaces. It was too dangerous.

Apologising, I said Lucy would have to come up front with me. Everyone froze. In Turkey, many believe that dogs are dirty and diseased, so for them, the idea of having a dog as a house pet is unimaginable and it is generally not accepted for dogs to travel inside vehicles either. In the countryside, older generations still believe that inhaling a dog hair puts the person at risk of cancer, a contemporary take on one of many safety stories passed down the generations to keep people away from dogs with rabies.

I knew it was a big deal to have a dog inside, and I felt awful putting the driver in that position. But I knew it wasn't safe to put Lucy in the back, and so I asked for my gear to be lifted back off the truck.

The hunters spoke to the driver; I had no idea what they said, but the driver finally agreed to allow Lucy to sit in front with me.

Deeply grateful, I lifted Lucy up onto the floor of the truck's cabin and climbed onto my seat. I offered to pay the hunters for their help, but they refused and said goodbye. I was so moved. Many people had refused to help us, or requested something unsavoury in return, yet these hunters, whom I didn't even like at first, went to tremendous effort to help us for nothing at all.

The truck driver was called Emir and was from Istanbul. He had been driving trucks between Italy and Turkey for 17 years and spoke a tiny amount of English. I pointed to the south of Turkey on my map and showed him where I had to go in Muğla, and he showed me the best and safest route. After that we rode in silence, with me mostly concentrating on the unfamiliar and wonderful feeling of sitting on such a big, comfortable seat. I gazed down at Lucy, who was looking back up at me. I thought about how I would love Lucy to have a home just like the dogs in Britain had. But we were in Turkey, and the sanctuary was the best option available. Watching her, I knew if I wasn't cycling the world and had a home, I would be her family.

$\barro$

Things kept getting worse between Mum and me, horribly out of control arguments and me wanting only to be in my room. By the time I was 15 she asked Social Services to take me away. She seemed to think that there was something wrong with me, and so I was sent to psychiatrists and psychologists. They said the problem did not lie solely with me, but the family unit as a whole. Mum rejected this idea. Things between us were miserable and tense, and I withdrew more and more. I went on living at home, feeling alone and unwanted. I coped by acting as if I didn't care, which allowed me to deal with a reality that was too much to bear – that I was so horrible my own mother did not want me.

Although I functioned in detached mode by day, at night when my bedroom door was closed, I cried myself to sleep. It was not only crushing, but also frightening. In the months leading up to my sixteenth birthday, I was deeply anxious, knowing this was the date my mum was no longer legally responsible for me. What would happen then?

I was studying for exams to allow me entry into university, and when I turned 16, I pleaded with Mum to let me stay. She allowed me to stay at home from Monday to Friday to help me continue with school, but I wasn't allowed home from after school from Friday until Sunday evening. She didn't care where I went, she just didn't want to see me.

I was very thankful for the arrangement, but my greatest fear was not finding somewhere to stay on the weekends, and that I would have to sleep outside on my own. This fear nearly came true when one Saturday night none of my friends could host me. My best friend,

Suzie, wouldn't let me be outside alone, so she told her parents she was staying at my house, and we took her tent up into the hills. It was the first time I'd ever wild camped. Unfortunately, it was winter and Suzie forgot the tent poles, so we spent a freezing night huddled together shivering in minus temperatures.

When I arrived back home late on Sunday afternoon, Mum was waiting for me, and she was livid. Apparently Suzie's parents had called to speak to her. Mum threw me out that day, screaming at me and telling me never to come back.

It was just before Christmas. I stood in the street, broken and completely alone. Numb, I began walking away from my home, away from my mum and my brothers. I didn't know what to do. I had only known life with my family. I walked some miles to a friend's house and her mum called Social Services. In the end, it was decided that I would live with a foster family 40 miles away. This meant travelling 80 miles each day to get to and from my school, but it was the best I could hope for.

Mum complained that she didn't want me in the same classes as my brother. Eventually, Social Services told me my mum was making a formal complaint that it was spending additional money on my school travel when there was a high school closer to my foster placement. I was told I'd have to change schools next term. I felt utterly panicked – I had lost my family; I couldn't lose my school and my friends, too. But I would.

Emir stopped at a junction where he would turn right and I left. He stood in the back of the truck, passed my gear down and said goodbye, driving off as I put my bicycle and gear back together. The road was quiet here, and I let Lucy walk beside me as I pedalled slowly.

After a few minutes, we stopped at a roadside restaurant, which had a big garden that looked perfect for Lucy. I had only eaten some bread in the morning and had fed Lucy only the hunters' breakfast leftovers. I grabbed my handlebar bag and entered the restaurant, smiling and motioning with my hands that I was very hungry and to please feed myself and Lucy.

I sat down at an empty table and opened my bag. My iPad was gone. This was a big deal because I used it to write my World Bike Girl blog. A few countries earlier, while cycling Bosnia and Herzegovina, I had the thought of writing a book about my cycling adventures and had begun my blog as a way of keeping track of the memories I was making, and also to improve my writing. I had no idea that so many people would be reading it. I didn't know when the iPad had been stolen or by whom. But I did know there was absolutely nothing I could do about it now.

It was late afternoon when we set off again, and we hadn't gone far when traffic police at the side of the road signalled me to stop. Lucy was sitting upright in her box, so I slowed gently before stopping in front of them. I leaned over, putting my arms around Lucy and telling her everything was OK. I spoke softly so she wouldn't be scared of the men.

They asked where I was going, and I explained I was cycling Lucy to a sanctuary in Muğla. They burst out laughing and didn't stop. I wasn't sure what to do. I stood there for a few minutes, and then finally just cycled away, leaving them laughing.

The road turned upwards. I was so tired. In every way – mentally, emotionally, and physically. Tired of everything. But I loved Lucy with all my heart. And that made the journey bearable.

CHAPTER 8

Darkness was falling, but I was still pedalling uphill with thick trees to each side, unable to find a camp spot. I stopped to take Lucy out of the box, put my headlamp on and switch on my rear light, hoping passing cars would see me. I cycled as fast as I could, but the incline and my exhaustion were both working against me. Lucy was walking beside, following me like a shadow. She was clearly exhausted too, and I felt bad that I couldn't have her in the box, but my headlamp was dim and there was too great a possibility of cycling over an unseen pot-hole.

Darkness fell completely and my daytime bravado crumbled, leaving irrational fears of the dark. My surroundings became like the wardrobe in a child's bedroom – fine in the day but scary at night because of possible monsters hiding inside. I longed to be safe inside my tent. I was glad Lucy was there because even though my heart rate and anxiety soared, I knew I would be a lot more scared without her.

My headlamp cast a tiny circle of light in the darkness. Was that a space among the trees by the kerb? I strained my eyes and braked. I could probably fit my tent there. I ran through my options: it was dangerous to camp here on this patch of grass so close to the road, and it was dangerous to cycle on in the pitch black, seeking a safer place to camp. Both options were especially dangerous in Turkey, where drunk driving is not unusual. The question was, which was the least dangerous option? With an attitude of 'better the devil you know than the devil you don't', I decided to camp where I was. I don't even know why I had stood deliberating; Lucy had already decided and was fast asleep in the grass.

I put up the tent in a panic, desperate to climb in, away from the menacing dark of the outside. I looked at sleeping Lucy. There was no way she could stay outside tonight. What if she ran out onto the road and a car hit her? She would simply have to sleep inside the tent with me. I felt bad about forcing her to do something she didn't want to do – and also wished I'd found that flea treatment – but it was a necessity.

I scooped her up, apologising to her as I strained my back muscles to place her inside the tent. I followed in swiftly behind and zipped up the tent so that she couldn't retreat back outside. I lay down in my sleeping bag cuddling Lucy, who was not impressed with the whole situation.

Each time headlights filled the inside of the tent, I was seized with a fear that a vehicle would mount the kerb and roll over us. I made sure Lucy was on the other side of me – silly as it might sound, I felt that I could offer her at least some protection if this happened.

I didn't sleep the whole night, thoughts spinning in my head. Three hundred and seventy kilometres. I didn't know which was worse, 370 kilometres of this hardship or 370 kilometres until I had to say goodbye. I decided the hardship was worse because, although I loved Lucy, I knew I could walk away. I was doing the right thing for her, and anyway, I was hard-hearted – Mum had always told me so – and I could cut bonds just as easily as I made them.

Dawn finally arrived, filling the tent with light, and I was thankful I didn't have to lie there, wide awake, any longer. It was only 6 a.m. as I sat cross-legged on the kerb, looking around me. The empty road was lined with tall, thin trees densely packed on both sides. At night this place had seemed a nightmare, but in the morning light it looked calm, peaceful, and safe. I tried hard to absorb this moment, so my subconscious could use it next time I got scared in the dark. Hopefully, with enough of these moments, I would become braver.

Although the day was only just beginning, I felt exhausted and every muscle hurt. Three hundred and seventy kilometres. I put my face in my hands. I couldn't do it. I couldn't face more dogs attacking. I couldn't face more men asking for sex. I couldn't face people pointing and laughing. I couldn't face another sleepless night. Now I was sobbing. Like the big cry-baby that I was.

It was in this state of desperation that I whipped out my phone and clicked on Facebook, posting a few photos of Lucy along with a plea for help. Even as I was typing it, I knew it was ridiculous. No-one would read the post, and even if they did, none of my friends had even been to Turkey. When I was done, I put my phone away and my head back in my hands.

Please help me & Lucy by sharing this post. I found Lucy being attacked by 4 dogs at the same time. Lucy only has 3 paws & couldn't run away. She just lay there. I got the dogs off & found Lucy a good home in Muğla, which was 550 kilometres away. I'm not allowed to use public transport because I have a dog. I built a box for Lucy, attached it to my bike & now we are cycling to her new home. It is day 4 & we have reached Balıkesir. Lucy is in pain from the travelling because of her injury and is so scared of the traffic. She has clearly been knocked down by a vehicle before. We have another 370 kilometres to go. We are on the D565 road to İzmir then we will be on the D550 from İzmir to Muğla/Dalaman area of Turkey. There are plenty of lorries & vans passing by. If you know of a haulier company or of a

*lorry/van driver going in our direction, please share our story. If you
know a bus company, please share our story. If you pass us & have
room, please stop. 370 km is not a lot to cover with vehicles; it is a lot
for a dog in pain. Share share share. I'm hoping this post will reach a
person who can help us on our way. Thank you x*

I lifted my head. There's no point crying, Ishbel. You learned that years
ago. Nobody is coming to help you. There is no way out of this other
than doing what needs to be done and getting to the other side of 370
kilometres. Lucy needs you. It doesn't matter how tired you are. How
much you are hurting. How much you think you can't do it. How
impossible this all seems. You just have to keep going. You have to
keep moving forward. You have to get Lucy to safety.

Using action to propel myself out of my mini-breakdown, I
jumped up from the kerb, woke Lucy, and began packing up before I
had time to think more thoughts. After all, 370 kilometres were not
going to cycle themselves.

I set off and was soon rewarded with the wide, flat, smooth hard
shoulder of an empty highway. No dodging pot-holes. No skidding
over gravel. No packs of attacking dogs. No lecherous men. And no
damned hills. With every pedal stroke forward, my energy returned
and my spirits lifted, and I was able to cycle all morning with Lucy
resting calmly in the box.

🚲

After I fled foster care, I was homeless and tried hard to go to school.
But being homeless and vulnerable won out. Years passed in a murky
blur of desperation, of unsafe company, subsisting hand to mouth, and
navigating in a dangerous underworld. I was 21 when I finally made
the decision to take back control, stop wishing I was dead and commit

myself to living. I bought a secondhand bike and cycled each day to and from college for the next two years, pursuing diplomas in holistic therapies and stress management.

The bike route from my apartment to the college was on a busy road with lots of traffic lights. I cycled as fast as I could, not because my bike was a horse anymore, but because I was disorganised and late every day. I took great enjoyment in sprinting from light to light, with cars as my competition. For the first time in a very long time, I felt safe in the world I was in.

As always, we stopped every so often for Lucy to stretch her legs, and today I noticed her limp seemed a little better. My legs felt better too, and our moods were high as we passed a nice-looking restaurant. I realised I hadn't had a proper meal in two days. The food I did have had been shared with Lucy, and I knew I was severely lacking in calories. I decided to stop and treat ourselves to keep in line with the first-class experience the tarmac was bringing us.

I had the chef cook a meal of chicken and rice especially for Lucy. It was so good I asked him to make it again so that I could take it away for her dinner. The restaurant staff were friendly toward Lucy, and I felt a surge of hope that things could eventually be better for street dogs in Turkey.

After I'd eaten my fill, I sat back and checked Facebook. I was astounded. People, lots of people, were sharing my post! People I didn't even know were sharing my post. While it still seemed unlikely that anyone could help us, it made me feel warm that strangers cared.

We got back on the bike, full and happy, and an hour passed without incident, which after the previous few days felt wonderful. No drama. No troubles.

Then a truck stopped ahead and a man jumped out.

I rolled my eyes; here we go again.

He stood waiting for us to catch up to him. I moved into the middle of the road in order to cycle around him. He asked, in English, where I was going. I ignored him and kept pedalling. He said he was driving to İzmir. I stopped. İzmir was 160 kilometres away! I waited, but he didn't ask for sex. I pointed to Lucy. He nodded his head yes. I waited again. He told me his name was Mustafa. Still he didn't ask me for sex. I showed him the Facebook post, which at that point was going viral. His eyes widened as I explained our story. I said that a lift would be very helpful, and I asked if I could take his photo and post it, so that everyone could see what a good man he was for helping us. His eyes lit up and he looked overjoyed. The fact that he was willing for his photo to go public on my Facebook gave me the security I needed. But nevertheless, when we loaded the bicycle and equipment into the back of his truck, I snapped a photo of his licence plate and messaged it along with my location to a friend.

He insisted Lucy get in the back with my bicycle. I checked out the container and found it safe. One hundred and sixty kilometres in this container was better than on my bike, and I agreed, provided we would stop frequently to check on her. He agreed. Once she was settled, I climbed into the cab and sighed deeply, grateful for the ride and for how much closer we were soon going to be to our destination.

🚲

After college and so many years of heartache, I set off to Australia with a backpack and a mission to simply explore and enjoy life. I took immediately to the excitement and the adventure. A year later, I returned and found an office job, which was less about building a career than it was about socking away money for more travel. I also began cycling with a local club. At first, I cycled mostly on my own because I wasn't quick enough to keep up with the fast group. But soon enough, I was keeping up, and word spread about a ponytail cycling among the men. One day a woman approached me and asked if I wanted to race on the team she was captain of. I thought this was ludicrous; I didn't know the first thing about racing and had no interest in learning. I declined, but she persisted, and other club members encouraged me to try. I finally succumbed, and soon after, I was road racing all over the UK as part of a women's race team. Cycling became science, and enjoying nature on my bicycle was replaced with goals of getting faster and stronger.

A velodrome was built in Glasgow to host the Commonwealth Games, and I decided to try it out. I stood in the middle, looking around at the high, sheer wooden drops, and thought, I can't do that. I was scared stiff as I stepped onto the wooden boards, but away I went and much to my surprise I was faster than everyone else in the taster session group. The coach for a competitive sprint team in Glasgow approached me excitedly, asking who I was and declaring he had been waiting for someone like me. I explained I road-raced, and he asked if I wanted to be a sprinter with them. I wasn't sure what sprinting entailed but had always disliked hill climbing, so I asked, 'If I'm a sprinter does it mean I don't have to race up hills anymore?'

'Yes,' he beamed, 'you don't have to race up hills anymore.'

'OK,' I said. 'I'll be a sprinter.'

I learned quickly and loved the discipline, the training and the racing. At my first big competition, I sped past the previous Commonwealth Games medallist from Scotland to take gold. I didn't believe it for a long time, but when I did I was so proud. Not because of my medal, but because of where I had come from.

We arrived in İzmir just as night fell. Mustafa pulled into an industrial estate where other trucks were already parked for the night. Normally, I'd never arrive in a city at night unless I had accommodation planned, but shedding 160 kilometres off our journey was a no-brainer. I planned on wandering the pavements all night, hopefully finding a bench so Lucy could sleep while I stayed awake, keeping us safe.

I lifted Lucy down from the container and then jumped back up and dropped down my bicycle and belongings. Once everything was back together, I thanked Mustafa profoundly and walked the bicycle and Lucy off into the darkness.

CHAPTER 9

In 11 hours, daylight would again invade İzmir, but until then I would stay awake and keep Lucy and me safe in a city of four million people. After so much time in rural Turkey, my senses were shocked at the bright lights, busy roads, and frantic speeds.

I searched through my pannier bags and found the white scarf I had used as a hijab in Iran. I tied it around Lucy's neck to act as a lead to guide her through the busy city. We dashed across a crowded road, and then I wheeled the bike with Lucy padding beside, continuing on to nowhere in particular. I had visited Turkey the year before after a sprint training camp in Iran and I'd met a Scottish couple, Caroline and Derek, with whom I'd kept in contact. They lived not far from İzmir and I had hoped to visit them whilst cycling Turkey but I knew that wasn't possible now with Lucy.

I spotted a towering sign displaying petrol prices at the entrance of a Shell garage. I noted the small area of grass that the sign stood on, as well as security cameras and plenty of staff, and immediately thought, *campsite!*

To find a piece of soft grass offering that kind of safety in the middle of a city was not to be passed up. The station was busy, with cars coming and going. I wandered casually across the forecourt, with Lucy walking beside me, and a goal to pitch my tent next to that sign. I knew it was best to hang out a bit before asking permission, to give them time to understand I had a good heart and was no threat.

Petrol stations in Turkey are famous among bicycle tourers for their hospitality, and within minutes of saying hello, I was drinking sweet tea. What did surprise me, however, was that the attendants were kind to Lucy as well, petting her and offering her bread. Their gentle attentions toward her were unexpected, as I'd noticed few Turkish people even touched dogs.

After finishing my tea, I asked to camp under the sign. The attendants' shocked faces told me they had never been asked that before. I explained that no hotel in İzmir would give me a room with Lucy, and knowing this was true, they agreed to let me camp.

Charging my phone in their office, I checked Facebook again and almost choked. My post was being shared all over the world. I had so many messages from people offering help, I couldn't read them all. Complete strangers – hundreds of them – had sent messages. One woman wrote, 'Get a taxi; I'll pay for it!' Others asked me to confirm my exact location so they could get help to me. One message in particular caught my attention; it included a phone number and a request for me to contact an English woman who was a few hours away. I called the number. The woman's name was Mary, and she ran a cat shelter in Turkey. She told me that she was coming to drive Lucy and me the rest of the way to our shelter, but she also said she was bringing the press because that way the news agency would pay and provide the transport.

She instructed me to wait where I was and to warn the station attendants that she would be arriving with a news crew.

I hung up, and my heart crumbled. I'd changed my mind. I wanted to scream that I didn't want any help because I wasn't ready to say goodbye to Lucy. But gratitude and common sense lifted me up from the depths of raw emotion. Lucy was safe. Within hours she would no longer be a street dog. She would be in a sanctuary with other dogs to play with. She wouldn't be harmed anymore. My Lucy was safe.

Just then – perhaps because I knew her safety had been achieved – a thought crept in. What about love? Who would give her love? One woman looking after a hundred dogs wouldn't have time to give Lucy love, no matter how big her heart was.

Amid the relief, my heart felt heavy.

I shared the news with the attendants, who were excited about a news crew arriving, but I didn't join in their enthusiasm. The task was done, and suddenly exhaustion hit me. I said goodnight and pitched my tent under the petrol sign, feeling sad. I loved Lucy. It had all happened so fast. I hadn't had time to prepare myself to detach and stop feeling. I was going to have to say goodbye. Oh God. I didn't want to. Tears filled my eyes, and I scolded myself for being silly. This is what's best for Lucy. I was cycling the world. I had only a bicycle and tent. I didn't have a home. She was much better off in the sanctuary.

I climbed into my sleeping bag and cuddled Lucy, both of us falling asleep straight away.

'Ishbel… Ishbel… Ishbel,' an English woman's voice called out to me in my dreams. Then my eyes opened wide and I checked my watch. It was 3 a.m. and the voice was real, not a dream. I scrambled to open the zipper, but Lucy was lying in the way and I couldn't get to it.

'Ishbel, it's Mary.'

I climbed over Lucy and unzipped the tent. I was blinded by a bright light shining in my face. I put my hand out to shield my eyes and scrunched up my face to see a woman with bright blonde frizzy hair and glasses.

'Mary?' I asked.

'Yes, I'm Mary.'

I grabbed her into a big hug, thanking her over and over for her kindness.

The cameraman was behind her with a big light, and another man stood with a giant fuzzy microphone. Mary looked past me and asked for Lucy. I turned back to the tent, calling her out.

The camera was still filming as Lucy appeared, and then she did something she had never done before. She strolled past, ignoring all of us, and with the camera trained on her, she squatted down to crap with her backside to the camera. God, I loved this dog. She was perfect in every way.

The cameraman had obviously been instructed to film the dog and there was an awkward moment as we all turned to him because it just wasn't right to film her going to the bathroom. Eventually realising, he turned the camera away and everyone burst out laughing. Lucy was my absolute hero.

Even though it was still dark, in the early hours of the morning, they wanted to see me cycling with Lucy in the box. I didn't like this. I had assumed that when I got Lucy to safety, she would never go in that box again. It wasn't something either of us wanted or enjoyed; we simply had no choice. But what could I say? These people were rescuing us.

I said sorry to Lucy and explained this was what we had to do in order to be rescued. I lifted her inside the box and began cycling with her. They wanted me to wave to the camera too. Don't they realise how hard this was with a fully loaded bicycle and a dog over the front wheel? Still, I did as they asked and cycled Lucy in the box, one-handed, waving with the other hand like a monkey in a zoo.

Afterwards, Mary, the television crew and I packed everything into their maroon van and set off. I concentrated hard on staying involved in the conversation, but I hadn't slept the past few nights and my eyes kept trying to close. Three hours later, around 8 a.m., Mary said we were close to the turn-off for her shelter and she asked about the sanctuary Lucy was going to. I told her the location in Muğla and mentioned Samantha.

A look of horror came over Mary's face. She shook her head from side to side and covered her mouth with her hand, her eyes wide. My heart stopped. I asked what was wrong. She turned away from me to face out the window, her head still shaking, a hand waving in the air and gasping for air like she couldn't breathe. My God, whatever it was, it was so bad she was having a panic attack?

I insisted, 'What is it? You have to tell me. If it's that bad, I can't take Lucy there.'

Mary started to breathe again. 'Ishbel, no! That sanctuary is terrible. Lucy won't survive there. If it had been anywhere else you were taking Lucy… but not there.'

Mary paused to look me in the eye before continuing, 'Look, I only have thirty dogs at my cat shelter and some have travelled to homes abroad. If you want, Lucy can come to my shelter; I will give her a place.'

'Really?' I could've kissed her. This was spectacular news. It hadn't occurred to me that street dogs could travel to other countries, and light bulbs started flashing in my mind. 'So, if I find Lucy a family in Britain, you know how to get her ready so she's allowed to travel to them?'

'Yes,' she replied.

She explained the procedures, and I said if Lucy went to her, I'd like her to have a full medical examination. I needed to know if she had anything wrong with her so that we could begin treatment. This was vital for Lucy, and especially important if we were going to look for a family for her in Britain. It didn't matter what the cost was; I would raise the money. Mary agreed and I hugged her, filled with gratitude.

I called Samantha and told her that Lucy had been offered a place at Mary's shelter in order to put her through procedures for adoption. Samantha seemed confused and said that Lucy could have gone through the very same procedures with her. I didn't mention what Mary had said about her shelter. I merely thanked her again and said that I would visit her once Lucy was settled. I felt bad since the whole journey had begun because Samantha had said she would give Lucy a place at her sanctuary. She was very important in all this, but Lucy came first.

We arrived at a town nestled into a peninsula of the Turkish Riviera and followed a road up into pine-covered mountains with panoramic views over Marmaris Bay, with its large green islands jutting out of the sea. The previous day I'd been cycling rural farmland; now I was on one of the most gorgeous coastlines I'd ever seen. We continued winding along the mountain road. A little while later, the car stopped and Mary jumped out to open a gate.

This was it. We had arrived. We had actually bloody arrived! So many times it had seemed impossible. I remembered willing myself to keep moving forward to this very moment of arrival. We had done it! Not only had we arrived, but there was a chance Lucy could have a real family soon.

I found myself choking back sobs. The last few days had been a journey of survival: I hadn't slept, and I certainly hadn't yet had the time or bandwidth to process any of it. I got out of the car holding Lucy, relieved but emotionally drained and exhausted.

I set her down and a few dogs came running over. Lucy was scared, so I held her close to me, trying to offer her a sense of protection. The shelter dogs were wagging their tails happily, but still Lucy pulled her head up, not wanting to engage. I felt nervous and uncomfortable myself, especially knowing that we were being filmed for television, and I wished the television crew wasn't there during such a personal moment. But then I told myself to stop being so selfish and to be grateful. This was what we had to do for the help we received.

Mary showed me around the tiny shelter. We passed caged areas with cats of all colours and sizes sunning themselves. Two horses grazed on a small grass area, and dotted around the grounds were individual kennels with a dog tied to each one. Lucy stuck close to my side as we walked, and each time dogs tried to engage her, she shrunk back into me.

At the back of the shelter was a tiny Portakabin where Mary said she lived. She explained that she really hadn't wanted to look after any dogs, but the local government, which supplied the food, pressured her to look after dogs as well as cats. So now Mary had a cat shelter with 30 dogs.

The press finally left, and I was happy to have some time to play with Lucy alone, but Mary said she was busy and that I should leave now. She insisted on paying for a hotel for me for the night and said that I could leave my bicycle and equipment at her shelter.

I didn't want to leave Lucy so soon. I couldn't tell yet if she was settled and OK. I asked if I could pitch my tent in the shelter instead or nearby. Mary said that wasn't possible, and that it was best for me to leave now in order to allow Lucy to settle. I accepted that Mary was the expert. But it was all so soon. Yesterday I still had 370 kilometres to go.

Mary assured me it was fine, and that I would see Lucy again the next morning for another television interview. I cuddled Lucy tight, holding my breath so the tears wouldn't escape down my cheeks. It broke my heart leaving her. I didn't want her to be scared. I didn't want her thinking I had abandoned her. I didn't want her sitting in her little kennel wondering where I was, waiting for me to come back. She trusted me.

I much preferred to wild camp as I always did, but Mary insisted I have a comfortable bed and hot shower. Her concern was very kind, and I finally agreed. Reluctantly, I jumped on the back of her moped and we descended the long hill to the empty streets of the resort below, missing its summer tourists.

We arrived at an expensive-looking beachfront hotel. We went to the reception desk and Mary requested a room. I felt extremely uncomfortable. I had no intention of allowing her to pay for a hotel room for me when there were so many animals in need, and I began walking out. Mary stopped me, explaining that a family had contacted her and donated £100 with the words, 'Get that girl a hotel for the night and a good meal when she arrives.' The money wasn't actually coming from her or from the animal charity, and so I accepted.

We said goodbye and hugged. A journalist was to collect me at 8.30 the next morning. Mary repeated that it was best for Lucy if I didn't spend time with her, that she needed time to settle in at the shelter. She suggested that I should return for her in four months' time, when she would be ready to travel.

I walked up the marble staircase to my hotel room and felt as though my heart was literally breaking. I loved Lucy, and tomorrow I'd have to say goodbye to her. I never, ever imagined it was going to be like this. Why hadn't I switched off, as I always had been able to in the past?

I had a warm shower and then wrapped a white fluffy towel around me and sat out on the balcony, overlooking a postcard view of the bay below with its long, deserted beach and beautiful green islands dotting the sea.

I focused on the positives. It seemed almost unbelievable that Lucy was finally going to have a family. The idea of it filled me with warmth. Although as a girl I'd cried for my family, later on I swore I preferred to be on my own, never tied down, loving my freedom and never even owning a goldfish. But as I thought about Lucy and her future, I knew I had been lying to myself for a long time. What I had wanted *most* was a family, to belong, to be safe, to have somewhere in the world that was my home. If I were granted one wish, it would always have been to have my family, and now that wish could come true for Lucy.

On the balcony that night, I wrote a Facebook post:

When Lucy was lying on the road next to my bicycle, the only option open to her was a good dog shelter. Now thanks to everyone on here showing love for Lucy & supporting her journey, we are going for the ultimate 'dog's life' for her. In 4 months' time, thanks to the Cat Shelter & their animal protection warrior Mary, Lucy will have gone through all the medical red tape to be flown anywhere in the world to a new family. If you are interested in Lucy being a member of your family, please message me and we will send you more info. This is Lucy arriving at her new home... for now. Let's get this right :-) x

I attached four photos to the post.

I collapsed onto the soft hotel bed and stretched out, feeling the silkiness of the sheets on my skin. I wondered if Lucy was OK. It upset me to think of her waiting for me to come back. But Mary was an expert. She knew best.

But did she? Experts weren't always right, and I had learned they couldn't always be trusted.

The year before I set out to cycle the world, I was focused on training to put in a qualification time to represent Scotland for velodrome sprint events in the Commonwealth Games. I had worked hard to get to this point. One evening, I was out for a cycle on the road and a car travelling in the opposite direction swerved across the road and hit me. I somersaulted over the car and landed hard on the other side of the road. Pain seared through my entire body. When I tried to stand up to hobble onto the pavement, the pain in both feet was too much. People surrounded me and took my arms to help me walk. As I was led into the ambulance, I burst out crying when I saw my expensive carbon racing bicycle in two pieces. The ambulance men told me not to cry because it could be me in two pieces.

After the accident, I suffered anxiety when cars were turning on the opposite side of the road. I was covered by British Cycling members' insurance, and their lawyer provided a therapist to deal with my anxiety. The therapist, a mental health nurse, was an expert in cognitive behavioural therapy, was published and had developed diagnostic tools that many psychologists used.

During therapy, he began discussing his marital problems with me. Within the first weeks of therapy he said he wanted to take me on a therapy week of cycling the French Alps, and wanted me to coach him. He said he thought he had fallen in love with me and that he wanted to have an affair because he didn't want to hurt his wife unless he was sure. For me, this was never going to happen – I knew what a broken family was, and I wanted no part of it. So he began to use therapy in an attempt to alter my thinking and belief system, telling me my attitude to the affair was an example of the black-and-white thinking that we had been working on. In one therapy session he said it would be helpful to practise chat-up lines but I refused, thinking this was ridiculous because I was not interested in meeting anyone and was focused on my sport. So he settled for my listing the qualities of a man I'd like to meet, and then in a future session insisted that the exercise showed I was referring to him, and he was what I wanted. All the time he stressed that I couldn't tell anyone because he helped so many people and if he lost his job, his clients would be affected.

By the end of therapy, I felt utterly destroyed. I reported him.

⚲

I left the hotel and went for a walk in search of food. I didn't feel like putting a smile on in a restaurant, so I bought a bagful of junk food from a little grocery store and went back to the hotel room. I had hoped that stuffing my face with comfort food would make me feel better, but it didn't. Finally I fell asleep, but it was a broken sleep with tossing and turning.

CHAPTER 10

The next morning, I awoke early, eager to visit Lucy. Eight-thirty couldn't come quickly enough. I enjoyed another hot shower but had no clean clothes to wear, so I dressed in my unwashed cycling ones. I looked in the mirror and had to laugh. Before cycling the world, I would never have gone on television wearing dirty clothes covered in holes. But now I didn't give a flip. There were more important things going on in the world than worrying about how you looked. Cycling the world was an entirely liberating experience and I loved the freedom and simplicity it brought to my life, offering a complete break from trying to fit in to society. I had space to just be me and my confidence was growing as a result. I loved that each day was so different, not knowing where I would pitch my tent each night. I loved not having a definite route or plan and be able to adjust my days at will, depending on who I'd met or the landscapes I'd discovered. I'd travelled many different ways and found travelling by bicycle broke down the most barriers that being a tourist brings.

I checked Facebook and saw a message in my inbox from a woman called Elizabeth. The note included a photo gallery of her house in England and a big garden, three ponies, a dog, a cat, and her young daughter, Abigail. She wrote that they would love to be Lucy's family. My heart melted. I messaged her right away, knowing already that they were perfect. We chatted back and forth, and

Elizabeth explained she was involved in animal protection back in Britain.

Sensing my bond with Lucy, she even offered to foster her instead until I finished cycling the world. This was fantastic news! It meant that I could cycle the world and then return for Lucy and somehow find us a home, and we could go for walks and be together every day. How was it possible that everything could work out so perfectly?

Then my heart sank. For you, Ishbel. Everything is perfect for you. By the time you are finished cycling the world, Lucy will have her home and you'll be taking her away from her family. If I wasn't prepared to stop cycling the world now for her, then I had no right to take her from where she belonged. I thanked Elizabeth for offering to foster but said that I knew her family was perfect to adopt Lucy and that I wanted Lucy to have her life in those photos with them. I meant every word of it.

Lucy now had everything: safety, love, protection, home and family. Feeling a profound sense of peace, I headed down to the hotel reception and checked out. The car and reporter were waiting outside.

I was elated to see Lucy. We collapsed into each other and spent several joyful minutes rolling around and cuddling on the ground. Mary explained that Lucy had been guarding my bike the whole time I was gone and wouldn't allow any other dog or cat to go near. She was so cute.

The reporters were waiting to do the interview. They took photographs and filmed me cycling with Lucy in the box. When the press left, I went back to playing with Lucy, knowing I would soon have to say goodbye.

Mary told me that the news station had asked her to take me to a shop and let me pick whatever clothes I wanted and that they would pay. I thanked her but said I certainly couldn't have money spent on clothes for me when I was standing in an animal shelter that was desperate for money. I explained I didn't need new clothes anyway, and that what I was wearing was perfectly suitable for cycling the world, but that I would be happy to buy the clothes if it meant that Mary could then sell them for funds for the shelter.

The fact that Mary lived in a tiny cabin inside her shelter pulled at my heartstrings. As we sat drinking tea in the sun, she went on to explain how she had no hot water, in fact no running water at all and certainly no shower. The fact that she devoted her life to helping animals yet couldn't have a shower moved me; I was awed by her devotion and sacrifice.

All the while I was listening to her, though, I kept thinking about the time ticking away, and how I really wanted to spend these last moments with Lucy. Finally, I politely excused myself from the conversation to play with Lucy.

It was time to say goodbye and cycle off, leaving Lucy behind. I wouldn't allow myself to cry; I didn't want Lucy to think that anything was wrong. I wanted our final moments to be happy and full of love. Dad leaving popped into my mind and the happy day at the park before he left made more sense to me. I gave Lucy a cuddle, and we remained in an embrace as she nuzzled into me. My heart was breaking. Why couldn't I detach? I forced myself to pull away and stand up. Mary held onto her, and I began pushing my bike toward the gate, tears rolling down my face.

At the bottom of the hill, I checked Facebook just to make sure there was nothing from Mary asking me to go back. I noticed that people were sharing link after link about people cycling the world with their dogs, as well as information about dog trailers that attached to bicycles.

Dog trailers? Suddenly I was walloped by serious second thoughts: should I go back for Lucy, and find a way to bring her with me? What about a dog trailer? Or a better crate?

But then Elizabeth's photo gallery came to mind, and I knew it had all worked out perfectly and that the family was much better for Lucy than I was.

I posted the news about Lucy having a family.

A wonderful family in the UK contacted me today offering Lucy the most perfect dog's life that I can imagine. There is Mum, Dad, a 10-year-old girl who's crazy about bikes, 3 ponies, a dog & a cat who are adopting Lucy. In 4 months' time, once Lucy has her international passport, I will personally deliver Lucy to her new family. I will raise the funds to enable this to happen. Lucy will love her new home, I am sure, but if she doesn't settle, I will go back for Lucy & she will be on a round-the-world tour with me. Every day Lucy was with me I had to fend off attacking dogs because she was travelling through 'their' territory. I don't want that for Lucy. That part of her life is over. I want her to be safe and secure at all times – she deserves it. It will break my heart that she is not coming with me, but it's all about Lucy – always has been. This family is perfect and we are so lucky.

I had made a plan to meet Samantha. She had arranged for me to stay at a small hotel, insisting that the sanctuary would be too noisy for me. We didn't know what time I would arrive that evening as I had 60 kilometres to ride, so we arranged to meet the following morning.

Leaving Lucy in the shelter had me thinking about my dad on that ride and I barely noticed the landscape I cycled through. I'd met my dad again at the age of 18 and he told me he had been a good father by walking away. I had believed him that he had been a good father but now I realised he was wrong. I had left Lucy in the shelter because I thought that was best for her, but I would always make sure she was OK and would provide whatever she needed. I thought of all the things I believed because my parents had told me, and for the first time I questioned their authenticity.

I arrived at the hotel just as the family was eating their evening meal and I joined them but was exhausted so retired to my room straight after.

I missed Lucy so much already. Before getting into bed, I placed her bowl and pink scarf on the cabinet next to my bed. I felt a little bit silly doing it and wondered what was happening to me. Lucy had changed me. I wasn't that hard-hearted girl anymore; I was even verging on soppy. As an adult, I had been on my own for large chunks of time and rarely experienced loneliness. Yet now, being apart from Lucy, I felt lonely for the first time. I thought of the Facebook messages about dog trailers and people cycling the world with their dogs. I wondered, again, whether I should have kept Lucy with me. But it didn't matter now; a wonderful family had come forward and would give Lucy a much better life than I ever could have given her.

The next morning, Samantha met me in the hotel reception. She was a large woman with red hair, and before I even said hello, I grabbed her into a warm hug. I owed her a debt of gratitude. It was she who had spoken the crucial words, 'I'll take Lucy,' that began our long journey. And it was those words that had echoed in my head as I cycled Lucy with so much pain in my body, at times just wanting to give up.

It was a beautiful warm day as Samantha drove me into the small town centre for coffee and shared with me how she had come to live in Turkey, and how she couldn't watch the dogs around her suffer. She had rescued a few desperate cases, but then became known to the locals as the woman who cares for dogs, and they began dumping dogs near her property. Injured dogs. Sick dogs. Nuisance dogs. Eventually she had too many dogs and had used up all her money looking after them. She now relied on help from charities overseas. I was surprised that Samantha didn't put her dogs up for adoption but she said they were happy there, running free on her land, which sat in the middle of a forest next to a lake, and in the summer the dogs could play in the water to cool down. It sounded like dog paradise.

I didn't tell Samantha what Mary had said about her shelter, but I knew she was confused about why Lucy had not arrived.

After coffee, Samantha asked if it was OK to drive by her sanctuary to collect paperwork before returning me to the hotel. I was excited to see this sanctuary where dogs ran free.

Some way out of town, we turned onto a rough dirt road and the air was filled with the barking of dogs. Several ran alongside the car, barking as we approached. She told me to wait in the car while she ran inside, as she didn't want them jumping up on me. I explained I'd be fine, but she insisted.

As I sat in the car, looking at the dogs racing around the grounds, any regret I had about Lucy not being here went away. This may have been a paradise for some dogs, but I quickly discerned that it wouldn't have been the best option for Lucy. Stray dogs kept in large numbers tend to pack up, and they don't like sharing their food with injured or sick dogs. In shelters where large numbers exist without separation it's common for sick dogs to be ripped apart because they have nowhere to hide. Staff have to be quick to spot when a dog gets sick so it can be segregated until it returns to health. I knew from watching Lucy being attacked on Turkey's rural streets that the chances were high she'd be bullied in a large pack environment.

Samantha dropped me back at the hotel and I stayed one more night, packing up and preparing for the next step in my journey. With Lucy at Mary's shelter, I intended to cycle across Turkey and into Iran. In four months' time, I would return for Lucy to take her to her new family in the UK.

However, I wasn't ready to cycle to Iran just yet. I didn't know Mary well, and I hadn't spent enough time at her shelter to know if Lucy had settled in. I wanted to delay cycling off for another week so that I would be available should Lucy need me.

The next morning, I stored my bicycle in the shed of the hotel and took a five-hour bus ride north to Çeşme to visit Caroline and Derek, the Scottish friends I'd met when I'd visited Turkey the year before. I was excited to see them.

Caroline and Derek were waiting at the bus station with big hugs and smiles. They had been married 40 years. I adored their vibrant energy and the way their eyes twinkled with youthfulness even though they were well into their retirement. Their wonderful sense of humour had me laughing continuously, which was a welcome break from the seriousness of the past week.

When we arrived at their house, they showed me to my bedroom and I sat on the bed to quickly check emails. I gasped out loud when I read the first one in my inbox.

I had known that an official hearing of the governing body to investigate my complaint about the therapist was set to begin in three days. It had taken a year to get to this point. However, the email informed me that things had changed. At the last minute, the therapist had changed his position to not guilty. He was clever, banking on the fact I was in Turkey and wouldn't be able to respond quickly enough. His plan might have worked too, but what he hadn't accounted for was me meeting Lucy. Somehow protecting and caring for Lucy had made me, for perhaps the first time in my life, want to do the same for myself. I thought about how I'd charged at those packs of attacking dogs, terrified but unshakable, and how neither of us, not Lucy and not I, were ever going to be victims again. Just as I had protected Lucy, I would protect myself.

Apologising to Caroline and Derek, I booked my flight immediately and arrived back in Scotland just in time for the hearing. I stood there, still dressed as a Turkish mountain woman, in front of a panel of suits and their legal jargon. For the first time in my life, I felt the power and strength to stand up for me, against a man who was powerful and respected, and declared I had done nothing wrong and that it wasn't my fault.

Though the therapist denied most of what had happened, I had supplied many text messages as evidence. The governing body's panel wrote a damning report and found him guilty of pursuing a deliberate and calculated course of action to instigate an inappropriate relationship with a vulnerable patient for his own needs, displaying behaviours that suggested a pattern of grooming. He was struck off from being a member of the governing body, which meant unless he proved he was rehabilitated and posed no threat to patients he would never be allowed to practise as a mental health nurse for any organisation that required governing body membership.

In all of it, the biggest shock to me was a report stating that my own personal history made me vulnerable to predatory behaviour.

How was that possible? Why had I never heard this before? Why had no-one ever warned me? I had never even considered that my past made me vulnerable to abuse as an adult. I knew if I was going to protect myself in the future, I had to understand and protect myself from my past.

I ended up staying two weeks in Scotland and found myself pining for Lucy. I hadn't heard anything negative from Mary to make me worry, but every night I woke up repeatedly in a fright because Lucy wasn't beside me. Then I'd remember she was in the shelter.

By this time, the British press had picked up on the story of Lucy, and we were hitting headlines around the world. I had asked Rachel and Eva, two friends I had made online, to go to Mary's shelter to take photos and videos of Lucy. They were part of a local animal group in Marmaris who had offered to help me and Lucy in response to my Facebook plea. Their video showed Lucy looking happy and seemed comfortable with the other dogs now. I was so relieved and grateful. As a way of thanking Mary, I tried to sell the last remnants of my belongings, to raise money for her to have a shower at the shelter.

I had posted on Facebook that my plane ticket back to Turkey was booked and that I'd depart Scotland in a couple of days. To my utter surprise, I received a message from Mum telling me she'd been following my blog and wondered if I wanted to meet before leaving for Turkey. My heart skipped a beat. Was this really happening? Having given Lucy a family, was I somehow in return being given my own family back? My friends were less excited and wondered why she would contact me now when she had not before.

I met her, and we had an early Christmas dinner together in a garden centre. We had been in and out of contact for several years but it had been a long time since I had seen her. It felt really good to

ABOVE LEFT It was winter when I first met Lucy. I was cycling a quiet road along the Sea of Marmara, 200 kilometres west of Istanbul, when I saw a dog padding behind me.

ABOVE RIGHT She was so thin her bones stuck out, and she had a badly damaged paw; and yet she ran as fast as she could to keep up with me, limping because of her injury.

BELOW Having been invited to take Lucy to a sanctuary 550 kilometres away, I had to find a way to put her on the bicycle, so I secured a wooden crate to the front for her to ride in.

ABOVE LEFT At first Lucy refused to sleep in the tent, keeping guard outside; then one morning as I brewed coffee, I turned to find her inside, fast asleep.

ABOVE RIGHT I had stopped at a petrol station in Yenice to charge my phone when I met a group of hunters, who went to tremendous efforts to help me.

BELOW LEFT At a friendly restaurant on the way to İzmir, I had the chef cook chicken and rice for Lucy.

BELOW RIGHT We stayed in Fethiye, the town where I'd first been inspired to try cycle touring. This photo was taken at Calis Beach, which became Lucy's favourite place to play.

ABOVE After receiving the bicycle trailer for Lucy, on 14 February I set off cycling along the south coast of Turkey. I was told by a vet to keep Lucy warm to alleviate any pain caused by the shotgun pellets inside her body.

BELOW Along the Turquoise Coast from Fethiye, the views were rugged and spectacular – navigating that landscape with a trailer was as tricky as any riding I'd done yet.

ABOVE and **BELOW** On the way to Antalya, the road reached the coast and became narrow and winding, up and down, digging into the vertical side of a rocky mountain with a sheer drop to the sea.

ABOVE In the mountains around Kaş. I was cycling a 90-kilo load – bike, trailer, luggage and Lucy – up and over hills on rough roads.

BELOW LEFT A shepherd boy, Toygar, invited me to camp near his farmhouse. Lucy played with the farm dogs while I helped him herd the goats.

BELOW RIGHT After a night of bitter cold and gale-force winds, Toygar's mother, Ümmü, prepared a breakfast of potatoes, onions, eggs, peppers and olives – perfect nourishment for the journey ahead.

ABOVE We coasted downhill and I stopped at a beachside café. The waiter came running over and showed me a photo of Lucy that he'd seen on Facebook.

BELOW With the threat of a rainstorm, I cycled 145 kilometres in one day to Alanya, where I managed to find a hotel that accepted dogs. We waited three days for the storm to pass, and in the occasional dry spell Lucy played on the beach.

ABOVE In the mountains around Kaş. I was cycling a 90-kilo load – bike, trailer, luggage and Lucy – up and over hills on rough roads.

BELOW LEFT A shepherd boy, Toygar, invited me to camp near his farmhouse. Lucy played with the farm dogs while I helped him herd the goats.

BELOW RIGHT After a night of bitter cold and gale-force winds, Toygar's mother, Ümmü, prepared a breakfast of potatoes, onions, eggs, peppers and olives – perfect nourishment for the journey ahead.

ABOVE We coasted downhill and I stopped at a beachside café. The waiter came running over and showed me a photo of Lucy that he'd seen on Facebook.

BELOW With the threat of a rainstorm, I cycled 145 kilometres in one day to Alanya, where I managed to find a hotel that accepted dogs. We waited three days for the storm to pass, and in the occasional dry spell Lucy played on the beach.

ABOVE LEFT Lucy playing in the tent while I packed up.

ABOVE RIGHT Children ran after Lucy, wanting to pet her. They were fearful at first, having been brought up to be scared of dogs, but a massive smile spread across the eldest boy's face when he stroked her head.

BELOW The schoolchildren here, near Adana, loved Lucy. A lecturer at Adana University invited me to speak to his classes, as he liked to show them different ways of living life.

ABOVE In Hatay, near the Syrian border, I was able to travel around by bus, in the boot with Lucy and she would sleep in the sun while I wrote my blogs in cafés. The last photo of us together was taken in the veterinary department of the university.

BELOW Lucy, I'll always love you.

see her. Yet strange too. She spoke cheerily and explained she hadn't thought about contacting me before but had been reading my blog and realised she really liked the girl writing it and had thought, *This girl who I like so much is my daughter.*

She said I had changed into a wonderful human being. I felt a twinge within me at that. I hadn't changed. Yes, I had matured like everyone else, but I hadn't changed. I was the same Ishbel I had been all those years ago. It seemed to me the only real difference now was that other people saw value in me and liked me. My blogging and adventures were popular and featuring in the press. That's what had changed. Not me.

CHAPTER 11

I flew back to Turkey in mid-December. The editor of an outdoor magazine in the UK had contacted me to write an article about cycling across Turkey in winter. Obviously cycling through snowy mountains in −13° C temperatures with a kit full of holes would be one hell of a challenge, but suffering always made good reading.

I'd have to set off soon in order to cross Turkey in winter for the article. Although I had agreed to Mary's request that I not visit Lucy, I simply had to make sure with my own eyes that she was OK before setting off on a bike trip where the most prominent aspect was survival. I didn't have any reason to think Lucy was not alright, but I wanted reassurance that she was comfortable where she was.

Derek had been for a medical check-up in Scotland, and it happened that he caught the same flight back to İzmir. So that night Derek, Caroline and I went out to celebrate. Life was good, I knew, but to really *feel* that life was good was a new experience for me.

Before I left Çeşme, Caroline bought me a notebook and pen so that I could begin writing my book. But in reality, writing a book seemed a tall order. Me, an author? It was a bold idea for me to believe, but I accepted the notebook and pen and decided to go ahead and think boldly.

As the bus pulled out, I waved goodbye to Derek and Caroline. I didn't know it, but that would be the last time I saw Derek. Soon after, he died of a sudden and aggressive cancer, leaving Caroline to continue life on her own without her best friend and life partner.

As I sat on the long bus ride, every mile a little closer to Lucy, I pulled out my new notebook. The first thing I wrote in it was an outline of my article for the editor. I knew this was a huge opportunity for me. Having an article published in a leading outdoor magazine would bring writing opportunities from other publications, which meant I'd generate income while on the road, every traveller's dream.

It was night when I arrived at Marmaris, and Rachel was there to collect me. She was an English teacher who had married a Turkish man, and they had three children. We had an instant connection, filled with that sense of knowing someone your whole life. I jumped into her car with the urge to tell her to go straight to Mary's to see Lucy, but it was late, and so I restrained myself and instead said hello to her daughter in the back seat.

Eva was Rachel's best friend, and she had offered me her spare apartment for as long as I needed it. She even loaned me her bicycle, since mine was still at the hotel, so I could cycle up to the shelter to see Lucy. Eva's apartment was modern and chic, and I told myself I wasn't going to sleep all night in order to enjoy such luxury to the full before the hardships of life on the road began again. Once I had made sure Lucy was OK, I would retrieve my bicycle and begin planning out my winter trip across Turkey.

Rachel, Eva and I got on well, enjoying a few brandies, chatting about life and animal rescue and laughing. I tried to set aside the agitation brought on by knowing Lucy was so close yet I hadn't seen her. Toward the end of the night, Mary messaged to say she had heard I was attending an animal fundraiser the next day with Rachel and Eva, and that she was upset about it. She said that she had a stall in another fundraiser nearby, which I'd known nothing about. She added that there was no way I could see Lucy in the morning because she was going to be too busy with her stall. Perhaps in the afternoon.

I drank more brandy.

I woke up the next morning with a message from Mary telling me I would not be able to see Lucy at all that day because she was too busy, and that instead I was to go to her stall at noon the following day. I was deeply disappointed. I asked her if I could just cycle up to the shelter early the next morning to see Lucy, promising not to disturb her in her work. She said no. I then asked if it was possible to see Lucy after she finished her work at the fundraiser. She again said no, adding that she was too upset to see me today. I had no idea what I had done wrong, but it seemed as if I was receiving a punishment.

Rachel, Eva and I went to the fundraiser as planned. Everyone there was asking how Lucy was. This was awkward because I genuinely didn't know. It also felt strange to be 'known'. Cycling the world solo meant I was always a stranger. But the story of Lucy and me was all over the press, and everywhere I went people knew me. It felt bizarre.

At the fundraiser, I began to hear stories about Mary, and the stories were similar to those Mary herself had told me about Samantha. No-one had a nice thing to say about Mary, it seemed. I knew to ignore tales unless I personally could confirm them to be true, but I was growing increasingly nervous that I hadn't seen Lucy yet and wanted to know she was OK. I was beginning to feel I couldn't trust what anyone said to me. I could trust only what I saw with my own eyes.

The next day I messaged Elizabeth. She, too, was on edge that I hadn't yet seen Lucy. I assured her that Lucy was fine, and that I would see her this very day even if I had to jump the fence. We discussed the possibility of Mary's shelter not being the best place for Lucy, and if that were the case, the practicalities of Lucy being with me for the four months. Elizabeth said she would begin looking for bicycle trailers right away, just in case. She sent me a photo of her daughter sitting in a dog bed and explained that Abigail was insisting on testing every single bed in the pet shop so she could find the most comfortable one for Lucy. Abigail and her classmates were also sending over toys to the shelter for Lucy and her friends for Christmas.

As agreed, I went to Mary's stall at noon. She was pleasant, but there was no warmth. I still didn't know what I had done to anger her. I asked when I could see Lucy. She said I couldn't today because she was busy with the stall. The helpers in her stall said it was no problem for them to watch the stall so that Mary could take me to see Lucy. Still Mary said no. Time passed and I hung around, not sure what to do. Eventually one of her helpers urged Mary to take me to see Lucy, offering to take me up herself if Mary could not.

Mary seemed to be fuming, but she relented. She and I got on her moped and headed up the hill to the shelter. I worried Lucy wouldn't recognise me because it had been three weeks since I saw her last.

I found her tied to a small wooden kennel outside. She was clearly ecstatic to see me, greeting me with licks, her head nuzzling into me. Time had done nothing to break our bond. But when I looked into her eyes, I sensed something wasn't quite right. I pulled her into a gentle cuddle and asked Mary if she had been OK. Mary said she was happy and healthy. She explained she had been so busy that she was a little behind schedule for Lucy being ready to fly to her new family. Again I looked into Lucy's eyes. They just didn't have the same spark as before. I wasn't sure what to make of it, or whether the stories I'd heard about Mary were right or wrong.

She began talking about bad storms and mentioned that a fence had been damaged, which meant the dogs had to be tied up all the time. I nodded and asked how long the fence had been damaged. Two weeks, she replied. I asked if Lucy had been tied to this kennel for two weeks. She hesitated. I waited. 'Yes,' she said.

'She was tied here in the storms?'

'Yes,' she said. 'I had thought about taking her inside, but I had other dogs.'

I knew how terrible and frightening Turkish storms were, as I had camped out in them many times myself. I felt sick imagining Lucy tied outside during thunderstorms. I stopped myself from saying anything, knowing there was no money in her budget for things like fixing fences.

We went to Mary's Portakabin where she made tea. She was acting friendly again as we sat outside, drinking tea and talking. Then she mentioned she had put one of the dogs in the shower room during the storm.

'Shower room?' I asked.

'Yes,' she said.

'You have a shower?'

She hesitated, realising her mistake. 'Yes.'

'But you said you didn't have running water?'

'I have a big tank that firemen fill up once a week. The water runs by pipes from the tank so it's not actually running water.'

'But you said you didn't have a shower.'

'Well, yes, I do have a shower, but look,' she grabbed a clump of her hair. 'Your hair is the same as mine, so you know that with our hair, a normal shower doesn't work well, and we need a power shower to get all the conditioner off. If not, it just goes all frizzy like this.'

That had to be one of the most ridiculous statements I had ever heard. 'Is it a hot shower?' I asked.

Again hesitation. 'Yes.'

'But you said you had no hot water.'

'Well, I have a generator but it's very noisy and sometimes it cuts out.'

This woman had told me she had no running water, no hot water, and no shower, and she now admitted to having all three. Disappointed and confused, I said nothing further about it and instead focused on Lucy, informing Mary that I was leaving today to sort things out and that then I would be back for Lucy.

'But I love Lucy, and she's more mine than yours now because I've had her for three weeks.'

Her voice started to rise, as she told me that she had been the one to rescue Lucy and me. In return she expected my complete loyalty to her. I was not to help any other animal charities, she shouted. I stepped back, surprised by her anger. Well, that explained why she had been so upset before and had tried to stop me from seeing Lucy.

She repeated, her eyes wild and her voice high-pitched, that she had helped me and this meant that I should help *only her* in return.

In that moment, I could hear my mum shouting at me that I was evil and bad and hard-hearted. I had believed my mum then, but standing here now, in the shelter, it was easy for me to hear the sadness in Mary's words. I felt concerned, not angry.

I told her firmly that her intimidation would not work on me, and that I would continue to help all animals in any way that I could. I repeated that I was taking Lucy and that everything would be confirmed and agreed with Lucy's adoption family.

Kneeling down next to Lucy, I said a gentle goodbye and gave her a reassuring cuddle. Mary was still upset as we rode on her moped in awkward silence back to her stall.

As I headed back to my friends' apartment, I thought about Mary's outburst and suddenly found myself for the first time asking myself if my mum's treatment of me had been much more to do with her own struggles than with me or things I had done. Maybe I hadn't been so horrible and bad. Maybe it had been my mum with the problems.

My decision was made. I contacted Elizabeth, explaining that Lucy would come with me on my journey, and then messaged friends asking for help sourcing a dog trailer and getting it to Turkey.

The next morning I did a television interview at the local dog shelter, which held hundreds of dogs. The journalists didn't seem to give a damn that I had cycled ten countries or rescued a dog. What they really wanted to know was why I was wearing Turkish trousers from the mountains. My answer, 'Because I like them,' seemed to confuse them even more, and the journalists looked at one another in shock. To them, it seemed ridiculous that a British woman should be wearing them because she liked them when they were hated by young women around Turkey, who absolutely refused to wear them. I looked down, repeating how much I loved them, and noticed I was wearing them inside out.

Afterwards, I said goodbye to Rachel and Eva and got on a bus to collect my bicycle and have coffee with Samantha. I had an idea to share with her. It seemed to me that if strangers on social media were willing to help one street dog, perhaps they would be willing to help many street dogs. When I took Lucy to her adoptive family in four months' time, perhaps the different shelters could come together to use that publicity collectively to drive fundraising efforts internationally for shelters in Turkey and put pressure on the Turkish government to improve the lives of street animals. Samantha loved the idea, welcoming any possibility of much needed help.

The next day I packed everything onto my bicycle and pedalled to Köyceğiz bus station in the hope of persuading a bus driver to take me, my bike, and all my gear to Fethiye. A friend, Paula, had opened her home there to Lucy and me until I managed to get the dog trailer. I found it remarkable that life was taking me back to the very town that had made me decide to cycle the world in the first place.

🚲

Kazakhstan grew smaller as I looked out the plane window, surrounded by my Iranian cycling teammates. I had trained so hard to get to this point, but I knew I was about to walk away from it all. The plane landed in Tehran, and I dumped my bike racing equipment back at the velodrome and booked the cheapest flight I could find, which was to Turkey. Grabbing my old training bicycle, a backpack, my bikini and wallet, I raced to the airport in a taxi. I arrived in Istanbul and caught a connecting flight down to the south of Turkey, where it was hotter and drier. I had no tent or jacket with me.

I had never been to Turkey before and knew nothing about it. I only knew that I needed time and space to decide what I was going to do.

When the Iranian National Cycling Team had offered me a place on their team, I'd jumped at the chance. I naively assumed that the team, being under the governance of the Union Cycliste Internationale, would ensure a level of professionalism and protection. But this did not seem to be the case, because every day the female athletes had to accept discrimination because of their gender. If we spoke out about it, we risked being thrown off the team. Perhaps because of my past and a commitment to myself to never be bullied again, I spoke up about the discrimination and bullying within the team, but nothing changed.

I loved racing but loathed the environment. I felt as though I was back in a world of bullying, dishonesty, cheating and fear. The world of performance cycling was for me a toxic place – too much like the underworld life I had worked so hard to leave behind. I'd put so much effort into getting to this place with my cycling, but now that I'd arrived, I found I really didn't like the destination. I had a hard decision to make: keep going in a world I didn't like because I had worked so hard to get there, or draw a line through it and try something else.

After landing in Antalya, I cycled the 200 kilometres to Fethiye, an upmarket, modern town on the Mediterranean coast. I was just locking my bicycle to a post when I saw a man with bright blonde hair and a red face walking toward me, pushing a bicycle overloaded with luggage.

'Hello,' he called out cheerily. 'I didn't know there was another one.'

I looked at him blankly. Just then a slim blonde woman on a bicycle appeared, looking unhappy. She looked at the man and said, 'You didn't tell me there were two of you.'

I looked at them both. What was going on?

'I don't know her,' he replied.

They both looked at me.

'Are you warm showers?' he asked.

Were these two crazy? 'Listen, I've no idea what you're talking about or who you are,' I said.

'Well, what are you doing here?' he asked.

I was so confused. 'I'm just locking my bike to this post, and then getting a bus to an office to change the date on a plane ticket from Tehran to London. What's the problem?'

They both burst out laughing as though what I'd just said was the funniest thing they'd ever heard. They explained that Warmshowers was an online community where people all around the world open up their homes to bicycle tourers passing through their area. The blonde woman was the host, Paula, and Jorn was the bicycle tourer, her guest. It just so happened that they had agreed to meet up at this very point at the same time that I had arrived to lock my bike to it.

Paula asked where I was staying that night. When I said I didn't know, she invited me to stay as well. Paula wanted to cycle from Turkey to the UK with her daughter, and Jorn had been bicycle touring for months. That evening I listened to them both talking about bicycle touring, and I knew in that instant that's what I was going to do.

I didn't even bother finishing my trip in Turkey. I pedalled straight from Paula's to the nearest airport, got a flight back to Scotland, and sold all my belongings for cash. Then I caught my flight to Nice to begin cycling the world with zero planning and zero preparation.

CHAPTER 12

'Let's go, Gareth is here!' Paula and I ran excitedly down the stairs and out to the waiting car, where a tall, lanky man stood waiting. 'Hello,' he called out in a broad Welsh accent.

Gareth had a jovial manner and an obsession with cycling. A few years before, he had retired to Turkey with his wife, Elaine, and they spent their time helping local street animal groups, raising money, dropping off food, and taking injured animals to vets. Since arriving in Fethiye, I had met so many wonderful expats who were involved in animal welfare. Gareth and Paula had become friends through a local biking group, and she had asked him if he could help me collect Lucy.

I was beside myself with excitement. We were going to get Lucy! We still hadn't found a trailer yet, to allow Lucy to ride with me as I cycled central Turkey for my magazine article. But it seemed there were none in stock in Turkey. Lucy's adoptive family in England were researching ways to get a dog trailer from Europe to here, but there didn't seem a quick enough way.

Halfway to Marmaris, a Facebook message popped up on my phone. It was from Debbie, who ran Dales Cycles, one of Scotland's biggest bike shops. She said she had been following my adventures online and asked for the make and model of the trailer I needed. I confirmed the type I was looking for, and a few minutes later she replied that her shop would supply the trailer for Lucy on the condition that I could find someone to fly with it from Scotland to Turkey. I couldn't believe this good fortune.

'We have a trailer! We have a trailer!' I shrieked, at a pitch that caused Gareth and Paula to jump.

All I had to do now was find a way to get the trailer over to Turkey. Gareth wasn't concerned, explaining that many British immigrants would be flying home to see family for Christmas so there was a high possibility of finding someone to bring the dog trailer back with them. He said he would put the word out on expat Facebook groups immediately.

We arrived at the shelter at 9 a.m. Excited and eager, I began calling Lucy's name as soon as we stepped through the shelter gates. She came bounding over as fast as she could and jumped up on me with a force that knocked us both to the ground and into a heap on the path. She went mad, licking me all over, her tail wagging furiously, and we got lost in a moment of absolute bliss. I couldn't remember a happier moment in my life than being reunited with Lucy, and it took me some time to get back up.

Just as I was standing up, laughing and brushing dirt from my hair, Mary appeared. I had been nervous about seeing her, uncertain how she would react after our last encounter. After what she'd said, I wondered if she might try to keep me from taking Lucy away from the shelter. I was thankful to have Gareth and Paula with me. To my relief, Mary was cordial and polite, and we spent a pleasant hour drinking tea and talking about her animals and the future of her shelter. When it was time to leave, I thanked her profusely, and then put a lead on Lucy and we walked out through the gates, just like that. A new chapter in our adventures had officially begun.

Lucy and I sat in the back seat of the car, and I cuddled her during the two-and-a-half-hour journey back to Fethiye, drifting in and out of Gareth and Paula's conversation about bicycles. It seemed like a dream that Lucy was sitting beside me. I wasn't quite sure what was ahead of us, but I knew Lucy wouldn't be outside, alone, in thunderstorms anymore.

We arrived at Paula's, but as we neared the entrance to her apartment block, Lucy pulled back hard on the lead. I tugged gently but saw her eyes wild with fear, and then in a blind panic, she threw herself down on the ground, lying flat so she couldn't be moved. Perplexed, I told the others to go on, that I would follow. I sat down with Lucy to calm her. You're OK, Lucy. You're OK. You're safe. Nothing bad is going to happen.

I understood the fear. Dogs were generally not allowed indoors in Turkey, I had learned by then that many people believe them to be evil and an expression of the devil. Even a dog walking past your house during prayer was said to interfere with the connection to Allah, and angels are thought not to visit if a dog is inside your home. Along with the prevailing idea that inhaling a dog hair can cause cancer, these ideas culminated in severe consequences should a dog attempt to go inside a building. I was sure during Lucy's life on the streets, had she gone near doorways, she would have been hit with sticks or stones or kicked, and if she had ever tried to go inside, she would have been taught a brutal lesson.

Lucy's survival had depended on following rules of the world she lived in. For years, Lucy had kept herself alive by not going indoors, so how was she to know now that these rules no longer applied and that it was safe for her to come inside with us?

I scooped her up in my arms and carried her up the five flights of stairs, my arms straining under the weight. In the apartment, there was a big dog cushion on the kitchen floor. I placed her on it and then sat on the floor beside her, stroking her back and giving her time to adjust to being inside a home, probably for the first time in her life. She remained still on her cushion, with a bewildered look, making no attempt to explore the apartment.

We stayed in the apartment for most of the day, giving Lucy time to adjust to being indoors. Paula and her two daughters were full of love, and Lucy responded with licks and a whirling, wagging tail. I took her for a few short walks around the block as well, and she seemed happy, eagerly discovering her new environs. Still, each time we went out, I had to lift her up and down the stairs. Not only did she refuse to go up, she also refused to go down.

Once outdoors, she walked calmly at my side, although whenever we passed a rubbish bin she pulled on the lead to get to it. Bins were a double-edged sword for street animals in Turkey. While they had food in them, which kept the animals alive, sometimes humans intentionally placed poison around the bins, which killed the animals painfully and slowly. Each time Lucy pulled toward a bin, I pulled her back. I knew it would take a long time for her to understand that she no longer needed to lunge at bins and gobble up everything she could get from them.

That evening, I carried her up the stairs to the loft area, where we would sleep. She was heavy, and it was all I could do to muscle her up the steep stairs in my arms. I placed her big cushion on the floor beside the bed. My hand dangled down to pet her, and I drifted off to sleep, feeling happy and at peace.

I woke in the morning to messages from Gareth saying he had already had three offers to bring Lucy's trailer over from Scotland. I couldn't believe it. I hadn't seen a lot of goodness in my lifetime, but since meeting Lucy, I had experienced an outpouring of compassion, love and kindness.

Since the offers were from people returning to Turkey after their visits home for the holidays, I would need to remain in Fethiye until after New Year's Day. Once the doggy trailer arrived, I could spend time getting Lucy comfortable riding in it, and then we could begin our cycle across Turkey. I was excited about writing my first magazine article. I had written to the editor, nervously explaining that I would be cycling with a dog, and I got the OK. Everything was falling so nicely into place – I wanted to pinch myself.

Knowing Lucy would be making the difficult journey across Turkey with me, I wanted to ensure she was as healthy as possible. The shelter in Marmaris had given her a clean bill of health, but I noticed that she still had a very poor appetite.

I took her to a local veterinarian named Selim, who came highly recommended. As we approached the office entrance, she pulled back on her lead, as usual, to escape the monster in the doorway no-one else saw. I leaned down and started to scoop her up, but Selim stopped me, explaining that Lucy must come inside of her own free will so that she trusted him. I glanced down at Lucy. She wasn't budging, and I was fairly certain that Selim would be waiting a long time for her to move.

He crouched down in front of her, speaking softly, and then stepped back into the clinic, kneeled down toward her again, and waited. And just like that, Lucy walked slowly inside the clinic to him. When she reached him, he smiled, gently putting his head down to meet hers and talking softly to her while rubbing her ears. I was impressed; this vet clearly had an amazing way with animals.

As he checked her over, I told him about her poor appetite. He recommended trying her on home-cooked food. I also explained how petrified she was of going indoors, which he had witnessed, and her refusal to walk up and down stairs. Selim said I should leave her to do these things by herself and not carry her. He was so confident and reassuring, and I left the office full of hope that Lucy would walk up to the apartment that night.

With Lucy walking calmly beside me on her lead, we headed towards the beach. We came to a busy road with traffic whizzing by. After some minutes standing on the kerb, I finally spotted a space in the traffic and we started across the street. We had almost made it to the other side when, without warning, Lucy threw herself onto her belly in a panic, pressing her body flat against the road, and lay still. I looked down at her and then back to the approaching traffic. My heart rate rocketing, I tugged on the lead. The cars were coming. I tugged harder on the lead. Lucy was petrified. She wouldn't budge. The cars were getting closer. I tried picking her up, but I couldn't get my hands beneath her. Eventually I got a grip under her, lifted her up, and jumped onto the pavement. The cars sped by.

I put her down, but again she threw herself onto her belly. I had no idea what was causing her such terror. She wasn't going inside, and there were no trucks. I noticed a small, fast-flowing river beside us. When she still wouldn't budge, I picked her up and walked over the bridge and river, placing her down on the other side. She then walked on as if nothing had happened. Had the river caused her paralysing fear?

We walked on, heading to Calis Beach – in our short time in Fethiye, this had become Lucy's favourite place. We came to a little wooden bridge over a small river, and once again Lucy threw herself down onto her belly, using her entire body weight in order to keep from being moved any closer.

I picked her up and carried her over the bridge, setting her down when we were some distance away. She walked on toward the beach.

I was certain now that Lucy must have suffered trauma involving water. I knew that it was common practice in Turkey for unwanted puppies to be put in bags and dropped in rivers. Turkish people rarely killed the animals themselves; instead, they put the animals into situations where death was likely, with a minute chance of survival, thus leaving the death up to Allah. If a tightly tied bag opened, for example, and a pup managed to swim to safety, or if a dog did not eat poison around a bin, then it was Allah's will that the animal live. If the puppies drowned or if the dogs ate the poison, that too was Allah's will.

While the reality for many street dogs in Turkey was a life of suffering, some Turks were working tirelessly to change that. The chairman of a Turkish animal organisation who also wrote animal protection laws had invited me to meet him in Istanbul to discuss how we could use the press coverage of Lucy to help shape a better world for street animals in Turkey. This was crucial work. The sole reason I had not yet agreed to go was that I was reluctant to make the 12-hour bus trip and leave Lucy behind.

At Calis Beach, Lucy raced about joyfully, jumping and digging in the sand. She played with other dogs and greeted passers-by with her vigorously wagging tail, seemingly free of the demons in her past. But when we returned that afternoon to Paula's apartment block, the demons returned, and she flattened herself on the ground again, determined not to budge. Inspired by Selim, I spent time gently talking to her and coaxing her with dog biscuits. Twenty minutes later I picked her up and carried her inside to the bottom of the stairs.

I set her down, wanting to follow Selim's advice and encourage her to walk up the stairs herself. She panicked, wildly trying to get back outside.

Finally, I picked her up again, defeated, and carried her up the five flights of stairs into the apartment.

Try as I might over the next several days, employing all my charms and a considerable number of biscuits, I couldn't get Lucy to climb the stairs on her own. Although it strained my back and stressed every muscle in my arms, I really didn't mind carrying her. But what did begin to concern me were the odd times – more and more as the days went by – when she became withdrawn and noticeably tired, and refused to eat. She had also peed twice on Paula's carpet, despite plentiful walks, and I noticed a swelling on her neck. Something wasn't right.

Two days before Christmas, we went back to Selim. He checked the swelling and sent some of her blood out for a rabies test. If the test showed she had sufficient rabies antibodies, she would be allowed entry into the UK three months after the test date. I spoke to Selim about my continued concerns about her health despite the bill of health from Marmaris. He suggested doing X-rays to see if perhaps her past injuries were causing her problems. I agreed.

He returned with several X-rays in his hand and a strange look on his face. 'Ishbel, what happened to Lucy?'

My heart jumped. 'What do you mean?'

He repeated, 'What happened to Lucy?'

I explained I only knew her history from the time I met her, seven weeks earlier. 'I'm positive she's been knocked down by a truck and they've probably tried to drown her in a river, so God knows…' I stopped rambling. 'Why?' I asked.

He hesitated, clearly distraught. 'She's got lots of shotgun pellets inside her.'

I couldn't make sense of his words. 'What do you mean, shotgun pellets?'

'She has been shot.'

'What do you mean, shot? Shot by what?'

'A shotgun. She has lots of shotgun pellets all over her body inside.'

He held up the X-rays and began counting: 31 shotgun pellets, in the head, neck, chest, hips, and knees. Many moments since meeting Lucy I had tried not to cry, but now the tears were rolling freely down my face. Someone had shot my beautiful baby girl. My heart broke for her. To have suffered that pain. To have been alone and scared. To be defenceless.

The X-rays also revealed that Lucy had suffered a broken hip and a fractured leg, and that one of her paws was destroyed. Selim explained that Lucy should not get cold because any drop of temperature would cool the shotgun pellets inside her and cause her pain. He said that this was why she became withdrawn and didn't eat. He also said that one of the pellets was likely pressing on a nerve, causing the swelling in her neck, and he gave me anti-inflammatories and painkillers for her. If the swelling didn't go down, he would perform a small operation to remove that pellet.

God knows what Lucy had endured in the years before I met her. I imagined her shot. Lying in excruciating pain. Bleeding, alone. This animal had known more pain and suffering than I could even imagine. I didn't just feel sadness for my beautiful girl; I felt a profound sadness for all the Lucys of the world, suffering alone in the streets. I decided in that moment that yes, I absolutely would travel to Istanbul to meet with the animal rights campaigner.

I walked Lucy back to Paula's and was glad it was dark because my tears wouldn't stop. I couldn't believe Lucy had been shot. I thought of what Selim said about the shotgun pellets dropping in temperature and causing her pain. There was no way Lucy could travel with me across central Turkey in winter.

Think, Ishbel, think. What were my options? Writing this magazine article was crucial to my continuing to travel the world on my bicycle. I knew I was being given a hugely valuable opportunity. Not only was I going to be paid good money for my work, but it would open doors for me as a travel writer. I didn't have any family to help me if I struggled. For all the risks I'd taken in life, I had to rely on myself alone. I needed to take advantage of this chance.

But what about Lucy? If she couldn't accompany me in the cold, where could she go? I didn't trust shelters I didn't know, because I'd heard awful stories, and at this point, I didn't have time to build trust with one because it was late December, and I had to leave soon if I was going to write about winter survival.

Lucy's well-being came first. She had been through enough. I had to protect her until I could deliver her safely to her adoptive family.

I knew I had to let the article go.

CHAPTER 13

Christmas Day, and for the first time in years, I woke up happy. I rolled over and reached for Lucy, who was still asleep next to the bed. I remembered past Christmases spent alone, opening presents that had handwritten labels reading, 'To Ishbel, Merry Christmas, Love Ishbel xxx.' Afterward, I'd ride my bike for a few hours on empty roads, listening to Christmas songs. On my return, I'd take a bubble bath, with candles and luxurious bath items I'd bought myself as presents. Dinner was always prepared the night before, knowing I'd be starving after my bike ride, and the ping of the microwave would tell me Christmas dinner was ready. Loading on pickles and pouring over gravy, I'd sit down with a tray to eat in my holiday pyjamas, watching festive television. I loved Christmas crackers, and I'd take one end in each hand and pull. I'd put on the paper hat and read aloud the joke to the four walls. After dinner, I'd settle into a bottle of port, and then the tears would come. Christmas was the only time of the year my mastery of detachment was unable to fully numb the sadness of feeling so terribly alone.

I watched Lucy sleep, rubbing her ears. Having her in my life made everything so much better; even today, the worst day of the year. It seemed no scars were a match for a dog's unconditional love.

I checked Facebook and saw that Paula was logged on too. I typed, *Good morning!* She replied, *Coffee?*, which made me giggle because it was 3 a.m. I lifted Lucy up onto the bed to give her big cuddles and rub her belly. It was Christmas Day and I actually felt happy! Paula arrived with mugs of coffee, and we sat talking about life until it was a reasonable time for adults to get up on Christmas Day.

After breakfast, instead of going for a bike ride, I decided to take Lucy for a walk to her favourite place, Calis Beach. It was a beautiful day along Fethiye's promenade, with luxury yachts bobbing up and down and bright green mountains dropping into the shimmering turquoise blue sea.

Lucy frolicked on the beach and was soon joined by two other dogs – both rescued street dogs, I came to discover after chatting with their owner. The three played like the happiest dogs in the world. Watching them, it was easy to see that the past didn't matter. In these moments, running free and happy, the past didn't even exist. The more I watched them, the more I wanted to emulate how they were adjusting to their new life, letting go of the past and living in the here and now. I knew that fears and scars from my own past still dictated much of my life. But I also knew they didn't belong in my life now or in my future. I had to let go.

On the walk back to the centre of Fethiye, I thought of Christmas Days when well-meaning friends insisted that I have dinner with their families. I always appreciated the kindness, but Christmas was one day of the year I couldn't bear being around other people's families. No-one knew that when I excused myself to go to the bathroom during dinner, I was sobbing my heart out. But today, with Lucy, I didn't feel sadness or that I was missing anything. I felt no fear, no need to protect myself, and no worrying I would be abandoned. I felt only love, and I basked in the feeling.

At dinner that evening, I wondered if I might get emotional, just as I always had in the past. But I sat at the table with Lucy at my feet all night, enjoying a wonderful dinner with Paula's family, feeding Lucy little tasty titbits, and not once crying in the bathroom.

After helping with post-dinner clean up, I crawled under the table and napped with Lucy. When I woke up, I slipped out from under the table, leaving Lucy asleep, and went to the living room to play with Paula's foster kittens. When I returned to check on Lucy, I found Paula standing in the dining room. She was upset. Lucy had peed again, she said.

I understood Paula's anger – this was the third time Lucy had peed on her carpet since we arrived. She scolded that this was unacceptable, and that I wasn't taking Lucy out for enough walks. I was as confused as Paula was, because I knew I had taken Lucy out enough. But I crumbled inside to hear Paula's harsh tone. I remembered Mum telling me how I had ruined Christmas Day. This was exactly why I couldn't be with a family, because I ruined everything.

As quickly as she'd got upset, Paula calmed down and apologised. I assured her that I was the one who needed to apologise, and helped clean the soiled carpet. The next morning, she brought up coffee as always and we chatted and smiled. And then I packed up, said thank you over and over, and gathered up my bicycle and Lucy, telling Paula that it was better if we left because I did not know what was wrong with Lucy, and there was a good chance she would pee again.

Paula insisted she didn't want us to go and that she loved having us. For her, the outburst about Lucy was forgotten as soon as she had apologised. But instead of hearing her, I heard only my mum's voice in my head, and I felt sure that Paula didn't want Lucy or me in her home.

I left Paula's place on Boxing Day, with a plan to wild camp for a night on the beach in Calis and then find a cheap bungalow to rent.

We hung out on the beach all afternoon, playing. Exhausted, we were just getting ready to camp when the sky turned black and an almighty storm rolled overhead. Before I had time to rethink our plan, big drops of rain began falling. I grabbed Lucy and then pushed my bike under the jutting awning of a nearby beachside hotel to stay dry.

We stood shivering under big, white letters that spelled 'VOJOS'. Unbeknownst to me, looking out at us through one of the hotel's windows were the founders of Animal Aid, a local charity helping street animals. I was just putting my fleece tartan cycling top over Lucy when the door opened and they invited me in. I recognised a few of them from a fundraising sale and I thanked them for the invitation, but explained I had Lucy and couldn't leave her out here alone. They told me not to be silly and to bring Lucy in too. Like so many others in the area, they knew Lucy and me from the press coverage and internet.

One of the Animal Aid founders, Andy, told me to wait a minute, and he went to speak to the hotel manager. He returned to tell me I was being given a room free of charge for the night, and that Lucy could stay with me. I nodded, touched and struggling to find words. Why were strangers helping us?

The storm raged all night, and I was thankful to be inside, cuddling Lucy. We stayed on at Vojo's over the next several days, and I began helping Animal Aid. Each morning I'd cycle around the street cat pods, feeding the cats and checking for ill health or injuries. Lucy liked to come along with me. She took no notice of the cats and was just happy to be out with me on an adventure. When anyone approached, she would wag her tail furiously. I remembered how when I first met her, I had thought her tail was broken because it stayed hidden between her legs. Now her tail was held high and was a constant wagging companion.

The holiday passed blissfully, with mornings volunteering and afternoons playing on the beach. Midnight arrived on New Year's Eve, and all along the coast fireworks filled the sky. Lucy ran off in fright, and I followed after her and found her crouching behind a tree, shaking. I held her tight, but she didn't stop shaking, and so I carried her up to our hotel room and lay with her. She continued to shake uncontrollably at each loud bang, which to her probably sounded like shotguns shooting from the sky.

Morning came, and the first thing Lucy did in the brand new year was to walk herself down the hotel stairs. Just like that. She walked down them with no coaching, no coaxing. And from that moment on, she walked up and down stairs with no concerns. This was a bigger celebration than the actual new year was.

On New Year's Day, I dressed up in a furry animal costume and joined others for a swim in the sea to raise money for local charities. Everyone knew Lucy and me, and bonds were growing. It was my first experience of feeling part of a community. I had moved around so much, I wasn't used to walking down a street and people knowing me and saying hello. I liked it.

Things were nearly perfect. Except that I was still worried about Lucy. Selim had assured me that Lucy's symptoms were caused by the gun pellets inside her, but I had an uneasy feeling. Something just wasn't right. Her behaviour was off; at odd moments, she would suddenly get testy, growling at other dogs and refusing to sit next to me on the beach, preferring to sit on her own. And she still wasn't eating well. If I didn't actively encourage her to eat, I don't think she would have. I wanted her to see the vet again.

Gareth collected us and we went to Selim's. The vet repeated that the trouble with Lucy was the shotgun pellets getting cold. I explained that she had been inside and under blankets in my room at nights, but he said that the metal would still be cooling even in milder temperatures.

So I began dressing Lucy in my fleece tartan cycling jacket. But I couldn't shake my worry about her. All the time, I was relaying information to Elizabeth and was relieved when she told me she had an animal behavioural expert who would work alongside her vet to make sure Lucy's transition into their home was as smooth as possible.

One day I spotted a pink wool sweater with the words 'Sweet Heart' written on it, in the window of a little charity shop. I cut the arms off and pulled it on Lucy. It fit her perfectly. This would keep her warm and prevent the shotgun pellets from getting cold and causing her pain.

When I posted a photo of Lucy in the sweater, I got an earful from social media. Some people loved the sweater, while others commented that it was disgusting to dress a dog up, and that they were unfollowing me. One follower pointed out the spelling mistake on her sweater. It turned out the words were 'Sweat Heart' not 'Sweet Heart'. Poor Lucy, to have a human like me.

A week into the new year, the dog trailer finally arrived when a couple flew over from Scotland and delivered it personally to me at the hotel. Although we no longer needed it to ride across Turkey for the magazine article, I planned to continue our travels together as long as possible, right up to the moment Lucy got the green light to go to England. The trailer was going to be a far more luxurious option for tandem travels than the crate.

Everyone was eager for me to put Lucy in it and go for a ride, but there was no way I was allowing her to try it until I knew it was safe – so I insisted on testing it on myself first. Much to the amusement and laughter of locals having coffee in the beachside cafés, I sat in the trailer as it was cycled up and down the promenade to make sure it was safe for Lucy.

Now it was time to put Lucy in the trailer. I was nervous. What if she didn't like it? I lifted her in, speaking softly as I clipped the lead inside to her collar. The lead would stop her from jumping out but was long enough that she could move around inside the trailer and lie down. She sat calmly where she was placed, her head poking out the head space. I continued petting her and telling her she was a good girl. Then I got on my bike, cast a reassuring look back at Lucy, and pushed down on the pedals. We were off.

Our first moments were accompanied by claps and cheers. I glanced back to see how Lucy was getting on, and she was sitting tall, as if she was the queen in the carriage and I was the horse. It was a beautiful moment, not only for us but for everyone who had helped make this moment happen. So many strangers had come together to help Lucy. I cycled up and down the promenade a few times and afterward rewarded Lucy with lots of cuddles and 'well done's.

Her test results arrived at Selim's office two days later. They showed she had enough rabies antibodies to be allowed entry into the UK three months later. This meant on 26 March we would be allowed to get the paperwork, which made her free to go to her new family.

We now had the trailer and the test results, and so in theory we were able to set off to continue cycling Turkey. However, I decided to hold off on departing Calis until February, when the weather was better and the storms fewer. When we did go, I planned to cycle east, hugging the south coast, because the weather would be warmer and thus better for Lucy's condition.

Vojo's was closing down – tourism had taken a hit in Turkey and many places in the resorts were forced to close – but a rescue volunteer I had met in Calis offered us a spare room in his home. So after a month in the hotel, for which the kind owners refused to take payment, Lucy and I moved in with Brian and his two dogs, waiting for the weather to improve.

Brian had retired to Calis, spent his time playing for a local darts team and was known for his frequent karaoke appearances. He had a beautiful five-bedroom, three-storey house with pools. Lucy and I both thrived on home life. Each night, Brian's two dogs followed him up to his bed, but Lucy never followed me up the stairs to mine. Instead she took ownership of a huge sofa next to the fire.

We were so content there, relaxing and going for walks to the beach. Lucy's appetite remained poor, though, and every few days I noticed that she became withdrawn. Given that she was in a warm house with a fire, I simply could not see how her symptoms were from shotgun pellets cooling down. So once again I took Lucy to Selim, but this time he said I had to stop bringing her in because he had already diagnosed her.

I felt bad to have bothered him so much, but still I couldn't shake the feeling that something was wrong with Lucy and it wasn't the shotgun pellets.

CHAPTER 14

On 14 February we set off cycling – me on my purple city bike and Lucy in her luxury trailer. I think she got the better deal! It was sad to leave our community in Calis, who had looked after us so well as we sheltered through the Turkish winter.

With my gear bungeed into pannier bags haphazardly, and the usual plan to sort it all out on the road, we set off from Calis at 2.30 p.m., which meant I pretty much cycled around the corner and then had to find a place to camp, as it was dark by 6 p.m.

I spotted a track to the left of the road. I stopped cycling and let Lucy out of the trailer so that I could push the bike over the banking and down the other side. We ended up in a grass-covered field that had panoramic views of snow-tipped mountains lining the horizon. I set up camp while Lucy explored the field.

It was a cold night, and though I knew Lucy would much rather have slept outside in the cold guarding my bike, to her absolute disgust I lifted her inside the tent.

I awoke at 5 a.m. to Lucy bolting through the wall of the tent – unsuccessfully. Realising she wasn't going to defeat the laws of physics, she then changed her game plan by running around the inside edge of the tent, with me flat on my back in the middle. It worked. I unzipped the tent and let her out.

It was still dark. A rush of freezing air shocked my face, and ice fell onto my arm. It was so cold there was ice on my tent! Apart from that time up a Scottish hill in winter when tent poles were forgotten, this was the most extreme camping I'd ever done. With ice on my tent, I was truly a real adventurer.

I quickly brought Lucy back into the warm tent, for which I received a paw to the jugular and dirt in my face in return. Charming. This was our first night camping again after Lucy had got used to her bed being a giant sofa, so I suppose a transition period was to be expected.

The morning's riding was cold, but the road was wonderfully flat, with little traffic. We pedalled along beside expansive green meadows lined with snow-capped mountains reaching up into a brilliant blue sky, and I enjoyed every smooth, easy pedal stroke, knowing all too well that it wouldn't last. Indeed, late in the day, the road reached the coast and became narrow and winding, up and down, digging into the vertical side of a rocky mountain with a sheer drop to the sea on the other side. The views were rugged and spectacular, but navigating that landscape with a trailer was as tricky as any riding I'd done yet.

Progress was slow, and before I knew it, it was nearly evening and I needed somewhere to camp. I passed some tiny patches of grass between the road barrier and the sea that I knew would just fit my tent; however, if I rolled over or Lucy tried bolting through the tent wall, we'd fall 100 metres into the sea.

A few more kilometres of pedalling and my concern was rising. Darkness was coming on in earnest, but there was no way I could cycle any faster with the extra 34 kilos that was Lucy and the trailer.

Finally, I saw lights lining the dark sea in the distance, indicating a town. I pedalled hard, wondering if I would make it before dark. Then, all at once, it was dark, and I stopped wondering. Bollocks.

A little while on, I came upon a fancy hotel with bright chandeliers shining through massive windows to my left. To my right, I spotted a little path into the woods. I decided to follow it and see if it offered a camp spot.

I let Lucy out of the trailer and wheeled the bike down the steep path. I arrived at a locked gate; beyond was wooden decking over the sea. I stood a few minutes looking around and listening for noises. It seemed totally abandoned. I looked behind me at the discouraging steep hill back the way I came and decided I might as well check it out.

I left the bicycle where it was and squeezed myself through the side of the gate, walking quietly across the wooden boards. In front of me was one of the most mesmerising night scenes I'd ever seen. The beautiful lights of a town lit up the other side of the bay, with black, gently rolling sea in front and dark jagged mountains behind. What a perfect place to camp.

I wandered around, looking for some grass on which to pitch my tent. I spotted a tiny bit on a raised bed beside an empty, white-painted beach bar. I wasn't sure if my tent would fit, but I was going to try.

I ran back to my bike, got my tent, and put it up quickly. Too tired to bother cooking, I tossed a few packets of crackers inside and crawled in. Lucy came inside quite agreeably, and as soon as we got into my sleeping bag, she fell asleep while I crunched on crackers and then fell into a deep sleep myself, with a spray of cracker crumbs in my hair.

I was jerked abruptly from a deep slumber by a light filling our tent and a Turkish man's voice shouting. I listened hard and could hear just one voice. I was relieved to know it was only one man, but he sounded very angry and was clearly not going away.

I unzipped the tent and was blinded by a strong light shining in my face. I quickly zipped the tent closed again, asking the torch to be pointed down. The man was still shouting in Turkish. I unzipped the tent and once more was blinded, zipping it closed again.

It was obvious that he didn't understand English, but I didn't know what else to do, so I asked again for the torch to be put down because it was blinding me. Still he shone the light. Finally I unzipped the tent, grabbed the torch out of his hand, and pulled it back into my tent. I peered out to see a stunned man looking back at me.

He began motioning for me to leave. My English was pointless, but I explained I was sorry and had run out of light and would be on my way at sunrise. He understood nothing and reached down to take the tent pegs out.

'Don't you dare touch my tent!' I said forcefully, more out of panic than bravado.

He froze at my tone. Then he took his phone from his pocket and made a call. I asked him for the phone. He said no. I was desperate. I absolutely did not want to go out there into the night. I held out my hand, beckoning for the phone, and finally I just grabbed it from him and put it to my ear.

'Hello,' I said.

The man spoke English. He was the owner of the hotel across the street. I begged him not to make us go out into the dark. When I told him I was on my own with a dog and a bicycle, he welcomed us to stay, apologising for his security guard. Relieved, I profusely apologised for trespassing and told him his guard was very good at his job.

Early the next morning, I wanted to pack up and leave quickly, out of respect, but took a few extra minutes looking out to the sea and islands. It was beautiful. The panic of the night before forgotten, I felt peaceful and grateful anew to be cycling the world.

A few kilometres on, we reached Kaş, a little fishing town built into a hillside on the Turquoise Coast. The streets were narrow and lined with jasmine. I had a coffee and then started the formidable climb out of Kaş at 9.30 a.m., following a winding mountain road through pine trees. To my great frustration, 11 kilometres later I was still pedalling uphill and it was already 4 p.m. At one point, a young boy came out of a house to the side of me and began strolling up the hill in front of me. I was so slow, I could not even keep up with his leisurely pace, so for my own sanity, I stared at the concrete under my bicycle until he disappeared from sight.

The difficulty and my slow progress suddenly filled me with doubt. Perhaps we wouldn't make our final destination, Hatay, which still lay 1,100 kilometres ahead to the east. Perhaps we wouldn't even make the halfway point of Antalya. I was cycling a 90-kilo load – bike, trailer, luggage and Lucy – up and over hills, some of which didn't even have tarmac roads, and I wondered what I'd been thinking to attempt to cycle all this weight on such a difficult route.

As if to match my mood, the clouds grew dark and a spot of rain fell onto my cheek. Bollocks. Now I wasn't even sure we would make it over this pass before sunset.

I passed a shepherd boy carrying wood on his back and shouted 'Hello' in Turkish. When he shouted back in English, I braked and asked him how far it was to the top of the pass. He said it was too far to reach today and that the rain was coming. Introducing himself as Toygar, he pointed to a white farmhouse with an orange-tiled roof sitting in the field beside us and invited us to camp.

Grateful, I wheeled my bike behind him and leaned it against the wall of his house. He then led me across a dirt field filled with goats, and after passing a duck pond, we came upon a short, stout woman dressed in baggy Turkish pants, thick wool sweaters and a dark-green wool hijab. He introduced me to his mother, Ümmü, who looked shocked at this foreigner standing in front of her. He spoke to her in Turkish, and a smile spread across her face.

We continued across the field, and farm dogs played with Lucy while I helped Toygar herd the goats. Just as rain started to fall, I set up my tent next to the house, and then followed Toygar inside. The family room was warm and welcoming, with white walls, a red settee, and a wood-burning stove in the corner that I learned was called a *soba*. Lucy had discovered a big couch outside beneath a roof outcropping that kept her dry in the rain. She stretched out on it, surrounded by her new playmates.

I watched Ümmü prepare dinner in the soba, hunched cross-legged on the floor next to it. She used a square of cloth to cover the carpet and a round metal tray to prepare the food, which was a delicious-smelling combination of potatoes, onions, eggs, olives, and peppers. As she cooked, I noticed her leaning to and fro to stretch her back, and she looked in pain. I didn't have the vocabulary to explain that I was a massage therapist, so I used charades along with her son's basic English to explain, making motions on her back while pointing to myself. I gave her a thumbs-up sign and then a thumbs down. She replied with a thumbs up, and so I moved her into position on the couch and massaged her back while instructing her son Toygar as well, so that when she finished working in the fields each day, he could do the same.

At bedtime, they invited me to stay the night inside. Before I'd met Lucy I would have welcomed sleeping on a bed in the warmth, but I couldn't leave Lucy outside on her own. Ignoring their protests, I insisted on sleeping in my tent with Lucy, and did an almighty sprint to get from the door to the inside of my tent because of the storm and dropping temperatures.

That night, it became painfully apparent that I had yet to develop sufficient wild camping experience in fierce weather to protect me from my own stupidity. I lay with gale-force winds battering into the side of my tent, knowing that if only I had pitched the tent on the other side of the house, I would have had calm and tranquillity, with the house acting as a wind shelter.

I had never experienced such bitter coldness. I couldn't even put my sweater on because Lucy was using it as a pillow. I lay freezing all night, wishing I were on the other side of the house and worrying about exposing Lucy to the cold. During the night, a dog outside kept trying to walk through the walls of my tent. It clearly was not comprehending that it was never going to make it, and I felt sorry for it. If it had just been me by myself, I would have brought the dog inside the tent, but I knew Lucy wouldn't tolerate it.

After a largely sleepless night, I was relieved when daylight finally arrived, bringing a bit of warmth along with it. I packed up quickly to get on our way. Before leaving, I was invited back in for breakfast, which was again potatoes, onions, eggs, peppers and olives – a perfect combination for the journey ahead. I enjoyed the moment of tea and warmth before having to face the cold that awaited outside.

To delay the inevitable, I sat by the fire, detangling my messy, wind-blown hair with my fingers. Suddenly Toygar appeared holding a hairbrush, and brushed my hair for me. It was a special moment: a belly full of good food, warmth from a wood fire and having my wild hair brushed.

We said our goodbyes and I cycled off into the cold, grey day.

CHAPTER 15

I had thought we were reaching the top of the mountain many times the previous day, but we never had. Today, just an hour after setting off from Toygar's house, we reached the top. I celebrated the fact that I was no longer climbing. I hated climbing, that was a given. But pulling a dog in a carriage, I hated it even more.

With glee, we coasted downhill, taking in stunning views of turquoise sea and islands. Once at the bottom of the hill, I stopped at a beachside café to get Lucy *köfte* (Turkish meatballs) for her breakfast. Our server came running over to our table. I was sure he was going chase Lucy off. But instead, he held out his mobile phone and pointed to the screen showing a photo of myself and Lucy that Toygar had posted on Facebook. The shepherd working a field in remote Turkey had Facebook? I smiled at my ignorance of an astoundingly connected world and sent him a friend request immediately.

The next few days brought steep climbs, snowy mountain vistas, enchanted forests and wild beaches. We were finally closing in on Antalya, which was significant for me. Many times, when questioning whether we'd reach Hatay, I'd struggled to imagine even making it to this halfway point.

I followed the road down into the bustling city with a huge smile plastered across my face. I headed straight for the supermarket, planning to cook up a feast tonight as our reward. Once out the other side of Antalya, I camped in a field down a dirt track. I never cooked meat for myself when wild camping. It was messy and attracted animals. Instead, I carried a mixture of beans and peas soaking in a flask, which I cooked instead. But Lucy still wasn't eating, so I started cooking breasts of chicken for her, which she seemed to like and was willing to eat.

I was staring at the stove with Lucy's chicken on it, fantasising about my own dinner, when my small gas burner caught fire. I quickly turned the gas off, but the damage was already done. I said goodbye to the stove that had cost me five dollars and had served me well through ten countries. Lucy got her dinner, but it seemed I was to go hungry that day.

As it turned out, hunger was not to be an option. A kind older couple miraculously appeared by my tent and invited me to their home for dinner. To be precise, the wife appeared by my tent, while her husband stood ten metres back in the field, not daring to take one more step toward us. With Lucy barking ferociously at him, the man's eyes were huge with terror and his face panicked.

Lucy was part Kangal, known to be outstanding guardians for flocks of sheep. Kangals never leave the sheep they are protecting and have been known to fight off even entire wolf packs. I'd heard a story about a sudden and violent storm that hit a Turkish village. The sheep were rounded into a shed for protection, and the villagers noticed their Kangal was not there. They knew something was wrong, because a Kangal never leaves its flock. They went out in search of the dog, eventually finding it lying in a field, and they thought it was dead. As they got closer, they saw it was breathing and that its eyes were wide open, but still it didn't move. When they lifted the dog, underneath they found a newborn lamb, which the dog had been keeping warm and sheltering from the storm. I supposed that Lucy's flock was myself, the tent and the bike, and she protected us fiercely.

I called her away from the man, but she remained in position. Finally, I walked over and took her in my arms, apologising to him for Lucy's behaviour.

The couple led me to their home, fed me, and invited Lucy and me to sleep in an unused apartment below their house, again moving past their own belief systems about dogs being indoors to ensure we were safe and comfortable. The next morning, as I prepared to leave, the woman brought out a scarf and tied it around my head into a hijab. She stood back, looking emotional with happiness. Once again, I was overwhelmed by the kindness of strangers.

We said our goodbyes, and I set out under menacing clouds. A bad storm was expected to cover the region for three days. I didn't usually bother checking weather, but Selim's advice about avoiding the cold for Lucy's sake was in my mind. I didn't want to expose her to three days of rain.

I could see in the distance a line in the sky where light prevailed. Today's mission was to out-cycle the rain, escaping the darkness by chasing the light. I knew by tomorrow there would be no out-riding it, so decided that tonight I would get accommodation for the duration of this rainstorm.

Stuffing my handlebar bag with a big packet of raisins, I rode my 90-kilo load as fast as I could all day. I didn't want Lucy getting wet and cold. The next town, Alanya, was 145 kilometres away.

Eight hours later, darkness was falling around us as we passed the welcome sign of Alanya. We had beaten the rain clouds! Lucy would stay dry another day. Struggling to believe I had pedalled

145 kilometres in a day with such a heavy load, I thanked my legs profoundly for helping me help Lucy.

Online, I found a hotel in Alanya that accepted dogs, unusual in Turkey, and I reserved a room. I rode up to the building just as the rain was starting to fall.

The storm lasted three days. We holed up in the hotel room, and during the occasional dry spell, Lucy played with the groups of beach dogs outside our building.

CHAPTER 16

The day began with Lucy fighting and it ended the same way for me, but setting off that morning from Alanya, we were refreshed and happy in ignorance of what lay ahead.

Early into the day's ride, we stopped at an expansive, beautiful beach. A large shaggy dog bounded toward us, tail wagging, with a big, daft, happy look on its face. Lucy jumped between the dog and me and showed her teeth. Suddenly the two dogs jumped at each other *Matrix*-style through the air, and an almighty fight ensued. The shaggy dog was bigger and stronger and had Lucy's ear between its teeth. I kicked the dog away with no effect. I then shouted at the top of my lungs that both of them would stop this fight immediately and would behave when in my company. Amazingly, they stopped instantly, walking away in opposite directions and laying down. Pleased with myself, I figured it must be the Scottish accent. No matter which language you speak or which species you belong to, a Scottish person shouting at you is terrifying. I checked that both dogs were unhurt and cycled onward, deciding there'd be no more beach stops that day.

Later in the day, the climbing began again. Today would turn out to be the toughest cycling yet of my world tour. Normally I used uphill sections for Lucy's exercise time, but this road was too narrow and twisting for her to be out of the trailer, so I suffered with the weight instead. I had cycled the full length of the French Alps and the Pyrenees and smashed out the infamous destroyer of cycling souls, Scotland's Bealach na Bà, yet I couldn't remember cycling such steep hills before. Undoubtedly, the combination of heavy trailer and heavier dog made them seem steeper.

I was cursing the road makers in my mind for this continual hell. But then beauty quelled my rage with the most superb cycling scenery I had ever encountered. Just me, my bicycle, and Lucy on a narrow, twisting road with a view of mountains covered in pine trees dropping down into brilliant blue sea. I returned to being thankful, knowing I was blessed to witness such magnificence of nature. Still, the road hurt, and so these hours were a strange experience of pain and pleasure.

I started looking for a place to camp well before dark. Cycling down the coast meant the single paved road was dug into the side of a mountain with vertical drops to the sea and tight hairpin bends. By starting my search early, I was sure I'd be successful. But I wasn't. Bollocks. It was going to get dark very soon. There wasn't anywhere to even park a bike, let alone set up a tent.

A truck lumbered past us and then stopped up ahead. I became wary. The driver climbed out and waved me over as I approached. He fuddled his way through a warning that it was getting dark and this road was not safe. I explained that I would stop soon, but he said there was nowhere to stop. It was like this for several more kilometres, he said, and there was another big hill yet to come. He said this road was dangerous during the day, and at night it was impossible. He offered to drive me to the next town over the mountain, where I could camp.

I didn't have much choice, so I reluctantly accepted the ride. I took photos when the bike and trailer were tied onto the back of his truck, but there was no mobile reception so I couldn't send the photos to any friends. I insisted Lucy come in front with me because then I knew he wouldn't try anything.

The man had been correct about the danger. By now, it was pitch dark and we were still climbing up the mountain road. I was thankful he had stopped. Eventually we arrived at the top of the steep climb, and I could see the lights of the town below where he would drop us off. He pulled into what must have been a small parking area on the hilltop. I couldn't see anything because it was so dark, but I could hear lots of barking, and then his headlights flashed on a pack of wild dogs just outside the truck.

I didn't know why he had stopped; I assumed he needed to go to the bathroom or perhaps stretch his legs. I thought him awfully brave to go out there with all those dogs. He turned off the engine, and I looked out of my window at the many dogs gathered, barking savagely at my door. Lucy was on the floor between my legs, looking up at me, and I petted her and told her what a good girl she was.

Instead of getting out, the man turned to me and said, 'Sex.'

'What?'

'Sex,' he said. 'Sex.'

I coudn't believe it. I'd never encountered this level of harasment anywhere else before. I looked at the dogs outside, then back to him, and shook my head very deliberately. 'No.'

'Sex or get out.'

'No sex,' I said firmly.

He was fuming now and insisted that I get out.

I looked at the pack of dogs outside my door. Jesus. There was no way I was going out there. I looked back at him. Jesus. There was no way I was giving him what he wanted either. Think, Ishbel, think. I had no way out. I had no mobile reception to call for help. I couldn't run or the dogs would get me. I felt my body tense up; if he laid a finger on me, I was ready to fight. I was strong after cycling 90 kilos day after day, and was sure that in a fight I'd take him.

I had dealt with many angry men wanting to hurt me in my life. I knew that the only way out of this was to take control.

I shouted with all my force that he *would* drive us down to the town like he said he would and pointed vigorously to the lights below. He shouted back equally angry, demanding sex. I roared back at him that he was going to do what he was told and he shouted back at me, 'Sex or get out, sex or get out.' I screamed back that I was not getting out, he was not getting sex, and that he was going to drive me down there.

He stopped shouting and stared straight ahead, the veins popping out in his forehead. Then he started up the motor, driving down the hill in silence to the edge of the town. He stopped and shouted at me to get out. I had no doubt he was going to drive off with all my belongings. I thought of all the effort that people had gone to get Lucy that trailer and I wasn't about to let it go.

I told him to offload my bicycle and trailer and that only then would I get out. The shouting match continued: he refused, screaming at me to get out. I yelled back no, that I would only get out when he offloaded my bike.

Suddenly he looked at Lucy, and his lips curved in a twisted, angry smile as he dialled a number and began talking in Turkish. He finished the call and got out of the cab. I sat still, with no idea what was going to happen next.

The Turkish army arrived. This was getting worse. He began talking to them and gesturing furiously at me. I sat where I was. I wasn't going anywhere until I had my bicycle and Lucy's trailer. A soldier appeared at my door and opened it, telling me to get out. I said not until my bicycle is off the truck. He repeated angrily to get out of the truck right now. I hesitated, and then told him to give me a minute to collect my bag.

He walked back to the group of soldiers and the driver. I didn't understand any Turkish. I didn't know what was being said or what was going on. I was terrified. I jumped down, lifted out Lucy, and began walking toward the men, tears rolling down my face. The soldiers all turned to look at me, and in an instant their faces changed from anger into concern. They turned to the driver. He was shaking his head. I shouted with force and pointed at him. Bad man. Bad man. Bad man.

The police arrived, and the driver was dragged off and driven away. They wanted my passport. My passport! I remembered I hadn't collected it from the hotel reception in Alanya. And now I was so stressed, I couldn't even remember the name of the hotel. Instead I wrote down my name and website on a piece of paper and asked the Turkish army to Google me. The soldier came back, having verified who I was using Google, and he had a military translator on the phone. Turns out the driver had told the army that I was hitchhiking. He said he had picked me up and that Lucy had attacked him and that's why he was asking me to get out. But then I came out of the truck with all my clothes ripped, and so they arrested him.

I kept trying to tell the translator that actually the driver hadn't ripped my clothes, that my clothes were just like that, but they didn't believe someone would be wearing clothes like that, especially a British person. They asked what I wanted done with the driver and I said I wanted his employers told, but they said he was self-employed. So, I agreed they could keep him in jail for a night.

They lifted my bicycle and gear off, and I put everything together and just walked away. A few hundred yards on, I came to a 24-hour restaurant and stopped. I went in, still shaken, and asked if I could pitch my tent there for the night.

They agreed, and I sat down to order food, suddenly absolutely ravenous. A Turkish family was sitting by the front door, finishing their meal. They began chatting to me. They had lived in America for several years and their English was marvellous. They ordered me soup and tea. They were friendly and warm and had such a wonderful sense of humour that they had me laughing within minutes, and I forgot all about the bad experience before.

In the morning, as I was packing up and thinking that I'd have to get my passport posted on to me later, the father of the family dropped off a new charger for my phone – mine had broken – and his wife gave me a beautiful stone ring for protection. They apologised for the truck driver and said there are many bad people in Turkey but they wanted me to know there are many good people also.

That day, the flat road I had been praying for greeted me, but with a headwind so strong I could barely turn the pedals. Embarrassed and frustrated, I wondered what people thought as I cycled alongside them at the same speed as they walked. I wanted to give in. I wanted to give in so badly.

I spotted a hill in front of me and a café to the side of me, and decided a coffee was definitely in order. I ordered my drink, sat down, and lay my wind-battered face on the table. When I lifted my head, they still hadn't brought my coffee. Then I noticed the time. I had been sleeping for half an hour. They brought me a coffee, which I downed like a tequila. Then I jumped up, put Lucy in her trailer, and attacked the hill as fast as I could to get it over with.

People always assumed I must be so strong to be cycling the world. But the truth was, many times I was only cycling a mile at a time. There were days that my body suffered and the road rarely granted respite. On those days, if I thought about the number of kilometres to the destination, I wouldn't make it. So instead, I concentrated on reaching the next kilometre, and I repeated this process all day if necessary, just to keep moving forward.

When I got into my tent that night, I didn't need to tuck Lucy into the sleeping bag. It was much warmer here than a few hundred kilometres up the coast. I lay in a state of exhaustion, windburnt and sunburnt, wondering what the hill was going to be like tomorrow. Would I manage it? I didn't know if I could do it. Would I give up tomorrow? Perhaps. I was so close to giving up. Would tomorrow be the end of our adventure?

I awoke in the tent at 4 a.m. with Lucy's big eyes staring back at me, her face inches from mine. I laughed out loud. I was so grateful for these moments and for the three-month waiting period she had to serve before flying away to her happily ever after. Once every day, I forced myself to imagine the moment I would drop her off with her family in England and cycle away from her. I hoped this would help prepare me for what was coming. I had no idea how many years it would take me to cycle the globe. I had no idea if the shotgun pellets inside her were slowly poisoning her. When I say goodbye, I thought, will I ever see her again?

CHAPTER 17

I began the next day with dread. The hill ahead looked brutal, even worse than I had imagined in my tent the night before. My dread was not unfounded. At times the hill was so steep that I could not turn the pedals quickly enough to keep the bike upright. So I would get off and push the bike up the hill, with Lucy padding beside.

At one point on the day's ride, a group of children began running after us. Happy for a rest, I stopped and waited for them to catch up. They wanted to pet Lucy, who was sitting calmly in her trailer, but each time they got close to the bike, they would become fearful and pull back. In Turkey, children are sometimes told that a big, bad dog will come and bite them if they are naughty. This was another of the 'safety stories' passed down from generation to generation, and served to keep children from going near rabid dogs. But as a result, children grew up petrified of dogs, and those fears often remained as they became adults.

I spent time showing them how much I loved Lucy and how to gently pet her. After repeated attempts to copy me and put a hand on Lucy without drawing it back, the eldest finally touched the top of her head. When his brother saw the massive smile that crept across his brother's face, he too reached out and put a tentative hand on Lucy's back. The youngest one tried to copy his brothers but kept jumping back, too fearful still to dare touch her.

I pedalled all day toward Mersin, which I expected to be a sleepy seaside town that I could bike right through to camp on the other side. However, as I pulled into the city just before dark, my misjudgement was clear. With just under one million people, Mersin was a dense concrete jungle, and I realised I wasn't going to make it out of the city before dark. The forecast for rain put a dampener on my 'sit on a bench and stay awake all night' strategy. I did a quick online search but couldn't find a hotel that would take a dog. Not sure what to do, we headed to the beach.

Generally I avoid beach camping unless it's in a rural or very secluded area, but I didn't have a better option tonight. I arrived at a café on the beach and discussed my situation with the employees, trying to gauge how dangerous it was to camp nearby. I was told a few fishermen would stand at the shoreline all night with their fishing rods in position but that I would be fine, so I pitched my tent in front of their café with their permission.

As darkness fell, a Kurdish man arrived. He warmly welcomed us and fussed over Lucy and me to make sure we were comfortable. He must be the café's owner, I thought. He insisted I re-pitch my tent inside the café's garden for ensured safety, which I did. When he laid down nearby, I realised that my new friend was not the owner. Rather, he was sleeping there just as I was, because he had nowhere else to sleep.

The next day I woke early and watched the sun rise, Lucy playing in the sand at my feet. Before heading out, I penned a note of thanks and left it for my Kurdish friend. That such a nice man slept on the hard floor of a café because he had no home made me sad. He remained in my thoughts for some time after I departed.

To boost my energy, I designated the day as Chocolate Day: after a quick stop, my handlebar bag was filled with chocolates. Chocolate

Day required a high level of bike handling skills, especially when the chocolates were individually wrapped. I cycled happily, my mouth full, through the smoggy morning traffic of Mersin's roads.

For our afternoon siesta, I set up my blanket on a small grassy area next to a football field. A group of boys dressed in football stripes were kicking a ball in the field. They spied me and came over, clearly curious.

I really wanted to sleep. Instead, I sat up and reached into my handlebar bag, took out the remaining chocolates, and held them out. They wanted the chocolates but had spied Lucy and wouldn't come near. I put the chocolates down and began petting Lucy, ruffling her ears and smiling, telling her how much I loved her. Then I picked up the chocolates again and held out my hand. The boys came over hesitantly, and I gave each a chocolate. They were delighted.

The biggest boy reached out his hand to touch Lucy. I nodded encouragingly to him and he patted her, tentatively at first, and then with confidence. As with our encounter the day before, the other boys watched the eldest touch her and then eagerly followed suit. Lucy was lapping up all the attention. I felt encouraged by these impromptu moments between children and Lucy, hoping the encounters might work to change their mind-set about dogs.

I noticed a few preschool kids standing near us, clearly uncertain about this monster they had been told might eat them. Each time I petted Lucy, they doubled over with laughter, as if they couldn't believe what they were seeing. Inching closer, they eventually were standing just in front of Lucy. They wanted to touch her too, as the older children had.

Just as one of them reached out his hand to pet Lucy's head, I heard bloodcurdling screams. I looked up to see a woman running as fast as she could across the field with a look of horror on her face.

She grabbed the boy up into her arms and pulled him away, then returned to save the other children, all of whom were now crying with fright. I sighed deeply. So much for a positive experience with dogs.

I packed up and put Lucy in her trailer. I cycled on to Adana, and just as I was reaching its industrial outskirts, I passed a police checkpoint on my right. The policeman waved me to stop. Bollocks. I still didn't have my passport. He asked where I was from and what I was doing. I explained, and he told me to come inside. I was worried, thinking he was going to ask for my passport, but instead he gave me tea and in return asked only for a selfie with me. And I was back on my way.

A lecturer at Adana University had arranged to meet me in the city. A keen cyclist, Zekireya had been following my journey online and emailed me a few days earlier to invite me to speak to his classes of students learning English. He said he liked to show his students different ways of living life and thought I would be an inspirational addition to his classes. He also loved dogs.

He and some of his students met me in a local park and then took me to a nearby restaurant. The students were eager to practise English, which gave me a break from playing charades.

Afterward, I was taken to a rented house where some of the students lived. It had been arranged that Lucy would stay on the balcony, which I knew was a generous offer, and I was appreciative of their hospitality. But when it came to bedtime, the students were horrified when I took my sleeping bag out onto the balcony to sleep with her.

As I lay there that night, I thought about how happy I was and about how much I wanted to keep Lucy. But I knew how selfish that would be. Lucy had the opportunity to have a real family. I pushed selfish thoughts out of my mind and imagined all the wonderful times Lucy had in her future. Elizabeth and her family were going to give Lucy the 'happy ever after' that I simply could not.

The next morning, the students gave me fresh clothes and styled my hair in a French plait. I felt beautiful for the first time in a long time. As we walked to class, passing students stared at Lucy, some confused and some shocked to see a dog strolling through campus.

I gave talks to classes about cycling the world, Turkey's street dogs, and how dogs are part of our families in the UK. The students fell in love with Lucy, lavishing love and affection on her.

We spent two days at the university, and just before the end of our last day, Zekireya presented Lucy with an Adana University diploma for being such a good dog in class. In a country where dogs were so often treated like vermin, to me this was a massive sign of hope. I was so proud of Lucy. She was touching the hearts of many and, in doing so, very possibly improving life for other street dogs along the way.

When we departed Adana, we had 215 kilometres to go to Hatay. Several hills stood between us and the finish line, but somehow it felt like we were – finally – nearly there.

We passed village after village as we climbed and descended, mile after mile. In one small village, Lucy was taking one of her exercise times in the day and walking along beside me. It was hot, and the climb had been steep, so I stopped for a moment's rest. An old woman wearing thick, woollen winter clothing was standing nearby and began throwing stones at Lucy. I was shocked and told her, 'No!' She took my hand and put a stone in it and made the motion to throw the stone at Lucy. She had a smile on her face. I dropped the stone and she threw another one. This woman thought she was helping me.

Angry and sad, I pedalled quickly away with a nervous Lucy trotting beside me.

I was facing the worst headwind of the trip, and although I was cycling with every ounce of energy I had left, I was going nowhere. When another hill appeared late that afternoon, I'd had enough and turned off the road, pedalling into the service station at the bottom and asking to camp. That hill could wait until tomorrow.

I was so hungry. I ordered food, and the kind manager had it delivered to my tent. I tried to give some to Lucy, but she only sniffed at it. My worries about her health were growing. I had been told time and time again that her symptoms were because of the shotgun pellets cooling, but it was so hot here, and yet she still wasn't eating. I had a bad feeling. I decided once I reached Hatay, I would take her to a vet.

The next day I cycled a hill, and then another one, and then another one. I was out of the saddle most of the morning. But finally, the road grew flatter and the towns bigger, and I began passing wedding shops with more frequency.

I had entered the province of Hatay.

CHAPTER 18

It had taken us 1,120 hard kilometres to arrive at this moment, and I took the time to snap the standard selfie against the Hatay welcome sign. I felt ecstatic and celebratory.

But that feeling didn't last, for it didn't take long to see the first signs of war.

I knew there was a war close by, but cycling past a Syrian Refugee Camp took me by surprise. It wasn't like those you saw on television. They, I later found out, had been full for some time, and so refugees were making their own camps, which farmers allowed on their land in exchange for labour. The refugees had tents for shelter but neither running water nor toilet facilities.

A group of children ran through the camp to reach me on the road, and I stopped, allowing them to catch up with me. Their small faces were streaked with mud, their clothes were tattered rags, and some wore no shoes. I said hello with a lump in my throat, shocked at seeing children so dirty. I had never seen such insufferable conditions. This was the first time children had completely ignored Lucy. Instead, they formed a queue and held out their hands, smiling at me. This broke my heart. I didn't have any money on me, not even change. I put my feet down on the pedals and cycled away with the children chasing after me, hands still held out in front of them. I decided I would stop at the next bank I passed to withdraw money. I never wanted to be in that position again.

I passed countless wedding dress shops. Men from all over Turkey came to Hatay to buy their second and third wives. Agents introduced prospective buyers to women desperate for safety. Such a booming business from the war resulted in towns being crammed full of these shops to service the human trafficking.

I didn't feel safe wild camping here; it would be a hotel tonight. After considerable searching, I found one online that would accept dogs. Following Google Maps, I started cycling toward the centre of Hatay. The road was a mess of pot-holes, and I grew wary as the area got worse and worse.

I cycled along the Orontes River, nicknamed the 'Rebel' because unlike the rest of the rivers in the area it flows south to north from Lebanon, through Syria, reaching the Mediterranean Sea in Turkey. The river reminded me a little of myself. Always going in the opposite direction of everyone else.

I finally arrived at the hotel, in a dirty and derelict neighbourhood. If Lucy hadn't been my bike's security guard, there's no way I'd have left my gear outside to go into the hotel. I walked in and was overwhelmed by the damp, mouldy smell. The staff reluctantly confirmed that they would allow Lucy inside, and I checked us in. They showed me to the room, and my skin crawled at how dirty it was. For sure I'd be sharing this bed with bed bugs. Still, it was a better option than being outside in the city at night.

I headed back downstairs to get my bike and Lucy when a manager approached me and said I wasn't allowed to bring Lucy inside the hotel because the other guests would complain. I nearly choked at the absurd notion that guests staying in a hotel where you could catch disease from breathing would complain about Lucy, who made no sound and was no bother. I argued my case, but to deaf ears, and was told firmly to leave.

Now I was back on the street, at night, in a town where I knew not a soul, less than 30 kilometres from the Syrian border. I had been told that the further south or east you got, the more people hated and feared dogs. I was now about as south as you could go in Turkey. As I walked along the street with my bicycle and Lucy, even grown men jumped out the way, petrified of her.

If I could find somewhere to stay tonight, we could leave Hatay tomorrow (never mind that we had pedalled 1,120 kilometres to get here). Facebook had helped me before, when I saw no options in front of me. Maybe it could help me again. I posted:

Saturday, 7 March 2015 at 10:47 UTC-03
I have a problem, reaching out to anyone in Hatay. The hotel is not accepting me with Lucy. Does anyone live in Hatay or have contacts who would be able to provide a garden or balcony for me and Lucy to sleep on tonight & we'll leave city tomorrow. Such a let down after cycling 1,120 km to get here :-(x

I kept walking and came across a Catholic church. I had gone to Catholic school and had always considered the church a beacon of safety and protection when travelling. I walked my bicycle and Lucy into the courtyard, which was surrounded by rooms for people who came and stayed to learn about God. I called out hello, and a man appeared and said there were rooms available, but that they would not allow a dog to stay. I explained Lucy's story, but he didn't care and returned to his office, closing the doors, leaving me in the courtyard in darkness.

I felt so alone and didn't know where to go next. I never would have imagined that the lowest point of my world tour would be sitting in the courtyard of a Catholic church in a Muslim country in a city just kilometres from the Syrian war zone. Being the cry-baby I was, I burst out into tears.

Then Facebook once again came to my rescue. People had shared my post, and it seemed two students were on their way. I was to meet them in a bar in the city's old town.

Lucy and I set off back into the night-time streets of Hatay. We entered the old city and wandered a labyrinth of winding, narrow streets. Passing silk-weaving shops and bazaars, we found the bar.

I popped my head inside. The students were watching for me and introduced themselves as Elif and Berat. Both spoke excellent English. Berat said that Lucy and I could stay with him. His apartment had a balcony for Lucy, he said, but no-one must know there was a dog in the building.

We left my bicycle in the bar for me to collect the next day, and walked to the bus. The driver shook his head and said, 'No dogs.' We pleaded, but once more he said no. The small bus, headed for the university campus, was full of students. Elif stepped on the bus and spoke to them in Turkish, and they all began calling to the bus driver to let Lucy ride the bus. He shook his head at first, but perhaps feeling outnumbered, he eventually agreed that Lucy could ride in the small luggage area in the back of the bus. The whole bus clapped and cheered.

I lifted Lucy into the boot and I jumped in with her, to the shock of the bus driver. There's no way I was letting Lucy be in the boot on her own.

We arrived at Hatay University and walked along the adjacent street of cafés and bars central to student life here. It was hard to imagine that only 100 kilometres away was Aleppo University, where 82 people including children had died as bombs dropped on the first day of exams.

Finally, we reached Berat's apartment, and I was overjoyed when he said he'd changed his mind and that Lucy didn't need to spend the night on the balcony. I slept on the couch, cuddling into her, my heart bursting with gratefulness and appreciation. The world was so bad on the news, and even on my trip I experienced the worst of human beings, but there was undeniably another side to the human story, and it was filled with goodness.

I woke up to a message from an advisor to the mayor. They had been told about my Facebook post and that a local hotel had turned Lucy and me away. They were trying to find me to make sure we were properly looked after in Hatay and invited Lucy and me to their home. I gladly accepted. Berat asked if I would come back the next morning to attend his archaeology class as they were discussing an ancient site in Britain.

Before departing Berat's apartment I laid out a quick breakfast for Lucy, but she would not touch it. I messaged Selim that I was very worried about her and that she still wasn't eating well and was losing weight.

We walked to the bus stop, and once again students protested and overturned the bus driver saying no to Lucy, and again she and I crammed into the luggage area to the sound of students cheering. Word was spreading about this curious girl and her dog.

We retrieved the bike at the café, and then Lucy and I cycled to the home of the advisor to the mayor.

I rang the bell at the gate, but when the couple appeared, they looked confused. I wondered if I was at the wrong home. All of a sudden I saw realisation spread across their faces. Laughing, they told me they had thought Lucy was a girl, not a dog. Luckily they warmly welcomed us both.

We enjoyed lunch, and, leaving Lucy in their high-walled secure courtyard, we went for a drive up into the mountains overlooking the province of Hatay and Syria and the sea to the horizon. We stopped at a mountaintop café, and they pointed out several areas of Hatay. They said I was free to go where I wished, but that some parts of Hatay were dangerous and that for those areas, they could provide me with an escort if I wanted one.

They invited me to stay the night. Honoured, I agreed. When it came time for bed, I began taking my mat outside and they asked what I was doing. I told them I wasn't comfortable leaving Lucy outside on her own, despite the secured yard. I simply didn't want her to be scared, I said. They said they understood, and insisted that we both sleep inside. I knew they were going against their own beliefs in order to make us comfortable, and I reassured them that we were both absolutely fine outside. But they would not take no for an answer. I thanked them profusely and accepted.

That night, Selim messaged me back, advising me to find a vet and get worming tablets and also to have her tested for digestive problems. My hosts told me that the nearest vet was 24 kilometres away. As I had been invited back to the university the next morning, I decided I would cycle to the vet straight after class.

The next morning I said goodbye to my hosts and cycled Lucy back to Hatay University. She stayed at Berat's apartment, while I attended the students' archaeology class and was delighted to find the day's lesson was on Stonehenge, possibly the best-known prehistoric monument in Europe. I decided I must visit Wiltshire and see it sometime.

Afterwards, I retrieved Lucy and walked to the main street. Leaving Lucy just outside, I went into a bakery to get something to eat before cycling to the vet and back. When I finished lunch and returned to my bike, I saw a girl kneeling beside Lucy, petting her and speaking softly. I almost choked. Someone petting a dog was highly unusual here.

I said hello. She introduced herself and said she was a third-year veterinary student at Hatay University. I explained that I was worried because Lucy was not eating, and that I was just then headed to the nearest vet, 24 kilometres away. She smiled and told me to follow her with Lucy.

It turned out that Berat's flat was directly opposite the university's veterinary department. The girl walked Lucy and me past security and into the main building. She explained our story to passing students as we walked, and by the time we got to the department head's office, we were surrounded by curious onlookers.

The head teaching vet checked Lucy over thoroughly, deduced that she had a bacterial problem in her tummy that had reduced her appetite, and gave me a prescription. Apart from that, he assured me that Lucy was healthy. I was flooded with relief. Surely my mind would be at rest now because here was another vet, the head teaching vet of a university no less, telling me Lucy was healthy.

The students took me to the chemist to get the medication and offered to help inject Lucy with antibiotics every day. Grateful, I accepted the offer. It looked as though we would be staying in Hatay a while, and thankfully Berat opened up his home to us until Lucy got better.

I shared the news with Elizabeth, and we agreed that once Lucy's treatment was finished, she and I would get a bus back to Calis; I did some research and found that I could take Lucy, sedated, in a crate in the luggage area of the bus. It was nearly time for her to fly to England.

Our time together was growing short. I soaked up the healing time in Hatay. Life there moved along at a slow pace, and I had nowhere to be but right where I was. It was a good feeling. Across from the apartment was a big field with long green grass, and every day I'd take a chair out to read while Lucy relaxed in the sun. The drugs seemed to make her tired, and I didn't take her for long walks as I had before.

Instead, we made short daily walks to the nearby internet café, where I would write my blogs and Lucy would sleep in the sun just outside. The café had floor-to-ceiling windows so I always had her in sight, and I could see she had touched the hearts of several schoolchildren, who visited her every day to pet her. She was soon well known to the shop's staff as well.

Each day I also took a few hours to absorb the region and culture. I was able to travel around Hatay as a student, which cost very little. I didn't have a student card, but all the bus drivers knew me as the girl who rode in the boot of the buses with her dog. One day I sat in a tea garden, reading an English version of the Koran and sipping on apple-and-banana tea, with the Mediterranean colours interrupted by bursts of smoke from students smoking nargiles – water pipes, a 500-year-old smoking tradition. It was mesmerising and peaceful. I was falling in love with Hatay.

CHAPTER 19

I had arrived in Hatay just before the refugee crisis exploded and a desperate mass migration of millions poured into Europe. Everyday life in Europe was not yet interrupted by the Syrian War, and so no-one really cared enough to help much.

The effects of war in Hatay, particularly on women, were clear. The official refugee camps in the region had been full for months. The refugees who made it over the border had to sleep in the street or build their own camps. There was great desperation. I heard stories out of refugee camps that babies were being sold for a dollar, and that teenage girls were selling their bodies for sex for the same price. It was getting to the point that women were not even being sold but were giving themselves away to men for free, to be looked after with shelter and food in return.

But at the university, life went on somewhat as normal. With the antibiotic shots finished, the university told me Lucy was healthy, and I went back to believing her symptoms were from the shotgun pellets.

I spent the Sunday of Mother's Day at the Syrian Dream project, where Syrian refugees learned arts, language, and social integration in one of the poorest areas of Hatay. The children showed off their artwork. They hadn't been to school for three or four years because of the war. Some children as young as seven years old were working six days a week to help feed their families. The project dedicated a special day for these children every Sunday to give them some of their childhood back.

Before I left, the children sang me a song, and I struggled to make sure that not one tear rolled down my cheek. I had no right to stand here crying when these children who had been through so much were holding their heads to the sky and singing out loud their joy.

I began Googling for more information about where I was, and what I read online was so different from what I was seeing right in front of me. The reality was much worse. All the agencies along the Syrian border were crying out to the Western world for more money and more resources, but they were being largely ignored. I decided to do the one thing I could do: tell their story, even if it was just to my own followers, because I knew they would donate and send blankets and clothes for the people here. I decided I would visit a refugee camp so they could see what was really happening.

The refugee camp was in Reyhanlı, an area I had been warned not to go to, not only because ISIS was said to be there but also because to reach Reyhanlı, I would have to cycle along the Syrian border. But the situation was desperate, and I felt it was crucial that I go. I decided I would start to cycle to the camp but be ready to turn back immediately if I thought it was too dangerous.

I made sure our student friends knew what time to feed Lucy in the flat, and I set off on a beautiful day with blue skies to cycle up to the Syrian border. Trucks passed me frequently, filled with soldiers and guns. I was petrified.

As the kilometres ticked by, I wondered if I would be shot. The fear kept building and building, and then, all at once, I changed my mind. I absolutely did not want to cycle to the refugee camp anymore. I was going to turn around and go back to Hatay immediately.

But it was too late; I had arrived in Reyhanlı.

I rolled into the centre of town, relieved to be alive. Cycling down the main street, I stopped at a shop with an English word in its window, hoping to ask for directions to the refugee camp. I lifted my bike up the stairs and tried the door, but it was locked.

A man came out from the barber's shop next door. He gestured that the shop was closed and waved me in for tea. I used Google Translate to tell him I was looking for the refugee camp. He was himself a Syrian refugee, he told me, and we continued chatting, haltingly, using the App. Finally, he called some English-speaking friends to come and translate.

The barber spoke about children tortured in custody, and their families protesting. He had already made one failed attempt to enter Europe on a boat with his family, he said. It had sunk, but he and his family were rescued. They were planning another attempt and were weighing which option they thought was less likely to have them killed: by sea, on overcrowded boats without life vests; or over the border from Turkey into Greece, where the chances were very high they would be shot.

He asked my opinion on which one was best, almost as though he was asking which local football team I thought would win an upcoming match. I felt shock and sadness.

People coming in to get their hair cut added their own stories of the war to his. They showed me photos of tortured dead bodies with black numbers on them; apparently there were thousands of them. I was told that most of them didn't die from the horrific torture wounds but from disease and starvation. I wanted to cry, but I held tears back. There was no place here for tears from a Scottish girl.

They told me about the start of the war; of the first nine months when they didn't fight back, waiting for other countries to step in and help them. Many family members were murdered as they waited for help. Finally they realised they had no choice: that to live, they had to pick up a gun and learn to shoot.

They asked me why no-one had helped them. They asked not in anger, but in disbelief and genuine confusion. They pleaded with me to record their stories. I explained I only had a little blog and that I was cycling the world. They didn't care. They wanted their stories recorded somewhere, if only to prove that they existed, they said, because they were all trying to get into Europe and no-one knew who would live and who would die.

I spent the whole afternoon at the barber's shop listening to refugees and aid workers. Evening was approaching and I hadn't even visited the camp, but I had to cycle back while there was still daylight.

Leaving Reyhanlı, I passed a young herdsman with a gun, herding his sheep. Walking beside him was a big Kangal dog. Around the dog's neck was a collar made of metal with jaggy spikes all over it, digging into the flesh.

I cycled on, sadness consuming me. What I'd seen and heard today was devastating, and I was struggling to process it all. I cycled as hard as possible, both in a bid to beat the sun going down and to release my emotions.

An old brown sedan stopped ahead. The driver got out and called to me, 'Sex – sex – sex,' pointing to his car. I exploded in a rage, screaming what a filthy, horrible man he was. Shocked, he moved quickly back toward his car door. Still I screamed at his back: 'Allah is looking down on you!'

He jumped in his car and fled. I cycled on, full of rage at him and at the war and at the world, which is probably the only reason I made it back to Hatay before darkness fell. I found out later that evening that a missile had been dropped 'accidentally' from Syria onto Reyhanlı. Turkey responded by dropping a few to send back a warning. Tensions were rising.

Lucy was in the apartment when I returned. I couldn't allow myself to be upset around her, and I enveloped her with love and affection. Then I went into the shower and I stayed in there for a long time, crying, affected by all the stories of human suffering I'd heard that day.

A few days later I received a call from the barber. He asked me to meet his wife and children. He said they were going to try another boat for Europe and he asked if they died, would I blog about their journey as refugees and tell people their stories.

It was arranged for me to go back to Reyhanlı. I returned to the barber's shop, where I thought I would be staying to listen to more stories. Instead, the barber asked me if I wanted to leave the shop and interview other people. I thought he must mean refugees, and so I nodded, and he led me through the streets of Reyhanlı to another barber's shop.

He said something to the man inside and then we all went upstairs, through a block of apartments, and the man knocked on another door. It opened and right away I knew I wasn't interviewing refugees. The man standing at the door was in a black suit and shirt. Behind him, I saw other men in suits standing around a table. The clothes, desk, and chairs were expensive-looking. There was clearly more money in this place than I had seen anywhere else in Turkey.

I took a deep breath and followed them into the apartment. They led me along a white-walled corridor into a large room with a huge wooden desk and sofa chairs positioned around it. The man sitting behind the desk stood and greeted us. Another suited man introduced himself as the translator. I was asked to sit, and as I did, I saw along the full length of one wall the words Syrian Revolution Command Centre.

They asked me repeatedly who I worked for. Each time they asked, I said emphatically: 'I'm cycling the world, I'm World Bike Girl, I don't work for anyone.'

They asked what I was doing in Reyhanlı, and I explained that I had cycled here to show my social media followers how bad it was, so that they could send blankets and toys and money.

Then the man said, 'We know about your dog, Lucy.'

I froze. *What the hell?*

'Can you tell us about Lucy?'

'What?'

'We'd like you to tell us about Lucy.'

'What do you mean? What do you want to know?'

'Everything. How you met her. What happened.'

This was ridiculous. Why on earth did these people want to know about a dog? Because I couldn't make sense of this turn in the conversation, for the first time that day I felt unsafe.

I began talking about Lucy. When I finished, everyone seemed astonished. We have thousands and thousands of people young and old being tortured and killed, and no-one cares, they said. But you. You managed to get a country that hates dogs to care about one dog. A street dog. We want to know how you did it. We need the same compassion for the people suffering in Syria.

I sat quietly for a minute. Then I said, 'The first thing you have to do is stop using the word *martyr* to describe a person who has died.'

This seemed to anger them. One man told me that even in British history, the word *martyr* is used.

I said, 'When we hear words like *mother* and *father* and *son* and *daughter*, we can relate. But when you use *martyr*, it's too far away from us and associated with a dangerous extremist world, and we switch off.'

I told them that what was happening in Syria was too much for us to comprehend, so we don't try. Getting the people of the world to care in a way that will make them want to march to their governments and demand help is only going to happen if you present the story to us in a way we can feel, I said. 'We are desensitised,' I said. 'You need to break through that.'

They asked what I would do.

I said if I were them, I would use a story about one child.

They asked if I would help them.

I thought about what was next for me. Lucy was coming to the end of her quarantine and would be going to the UK to be with her family. I would be back to having no-one. I was deeply affected by the human and animal suffering I had experienced while cycling across Turkey, and, I thought, if there was even a minute chance I could help save people from the horrible deaths I saw in those photos, then, yes, of course I would help.

They asked me to write stories that would connect with the hearts of the world. The plan would be for escorts to first drive me around the refugee camps on the Turkish side, where I could interview people. After that, if I felt it was necessary, we could go into Syria.

The meeting ended, and I was taken to meet their leader. We all sat in a circle around his office. He told me Bashar al-Assad's men were using chemical weapons and showed me live feeds coming out of Syria. He had tears in his eyes. 'Why is no-one doing anything about the chemical attacks?' he asked. I had no answer for him. I didn't know a Goddamned thing. About anything. I was just riding a bicycle around the world. But one thing I knew. Once Lucy was with her new family, I was coming back to go into Syria.

CHAPTER 20

The next day was Lucy's last day of quarantine. At last I could apply for her paperwork allowing her entry into the UK. Her adoptive family was so excited. I even messaged Selim the happy news.

I stepped out of the internet café and walked back to the apartment. I knew instantly something was wrong. Lucy hadn't jumped up to be by my side. She remained where she was.

I went over and was petting her and encouraging her to come, but she would not get up. I stepped away again, calling her and clapping my hands on my knees. She reluctantly got up and walked a few steps toward me. Something was very wrong.

I walked slowly with her, back along the main street and through the big archways of the university, the security guard giving us a wave and a smile. I knocked on the admin door of the veterinary department. The assistant was happy to see us again. I explained about Lucy and he asked me to bring her in.

She still would never willingly walk indoors, so I lifted her and placed her on a metal surgical table. I waited for some time, and finally the director of the department and the head teaching vet arrived. Lucy was quite a famous dog in Turkey now and as such was offered VIP treatment. I was so thankful.

They examined Lucy, asking me what was wrong. I explained that she didn't come to my side and she was walking very slowly. She wasn't breathing right. Lucy let out a little yelp when she was touched in the tummy. My face contorted. They finished their examination and told me everything was OK.

'But she's sick,' I said.

'No, no, it's just a cold, probably from the change in weather because it's so hot here and up where you came from it's cold.'

'But she yelped when you examined her,' I insisted.

'No, no, trust us. We've examined her thoroughly, and she's fine.'

The director faced me square on and said, 'Don't worry, Ishbel, she is OK, it's just a dog cold.'

They seemed so sure. And they were top vets in the country.

I left with Lucy, still worried, and carried her all the way home. I made her chicken, but she wouldn't eat it. I messaged Selim that I had taken Lucy to the veterinary department again today. I listed her issues: she does not have a temperature but her breathing is not right, she has a runny nose, her belly seems swollen, she does not want to walk.

I looked up from messaging Selim, and Lucy was standing at the closed door to go outside. Suddenly, she threw up. It was yellow. I comforted her and cleaned it up. Then I messaged Selim again to tell him what had happened.

He advised me not to feed her until the next evening, and then for two days only chicken and rice.

As the night went on, Lucy worsened. I lifted her out onto the balcony for some fresh air, but her breathing didn't improve. So I carried her down the stairs, out of the apartment, and into the darkness. I carried her across the path and into the field we played in, and there I laid her down. I ran back upstairs and grabbed a chair, sweater, hat, and a book and ran back down. I set down my chair with Lucy lying beside me. I brought the book because that's what people did when they waited; they read a book. But I was in darkness, without a torch. And so I just sat and waited. And waited. All the while stroking Lucy gently, telling her what a good dog she was.

Lightness came and she could hardly breathe, there was black goo coming from her behind. I had no idea what to do. There were no emergency vets to call, no vet hospital in town. I had only the university and it didn't open until 8 a.m.

Lucy's tummy was even more swollen. Selim messaged, saying to take her to the veterinary department at the university and to ask for a barium X-ray, as she may have a blockage or twisted tummy or intestine.

I noticed black liquid coming out of her mouth. I picked her up and began walking along the street. She was so heavy in my arms. The black stuff coming out of her mouth and bum was covering me.

Oh my God, she was so heavy. I was going to drop her. I put my head to the heavens, my face twisted in pain, and I prayed for the strength to carry her, tears rolling down my face. My beautiful baby.

I had to put her down for a moment or I knew I would drop her. I saw two small boys with a trailer nearby, rummaging around in a big bin. I stumbled over and lay Lucy down. The boys were black with dirt, their clothes dirty and full of holes, and they looked frightened. I begged them to lend me their trailer to take my dog to the vet, promising I would bring it back. But they didn't understand.

A young man coming out of his house saw me standing, sobbing to the street children, and he walked over. He spoke a little English, so I explained. He understood enough and he asked the boys in Turkish for their trailer. They shook their heads no, looking at Lucy.

The man, whom I had never met before, took out his wallet and offered them money. Still they refused.

Lucy was still lying on the concrete. Another man came out of the apartment building and called over, saying said he would drive us. I picked Lucy up and moved to place her into the back seat, but he stopped me and opened the boot, instructing me to put her there. My heart sank. I didn't want Lucy on her own in the boot of a car. But I knew we had no choice.

After what felt like the longest journey I'd ever taken but was probably only a couple of minutes, we reached the university. He stopped outside the veterinary department, and I picked Lucy out of the boot and headed straight into the corridor.

The receptionist came out of his office. I told him Lucy was sick and that I needed a vet now. He brought me into the surgery room and asked to lay Lucy down on the steel trolley. A few students came in too – Lucy had a lot of friends in the university.

She was getting worse. I kept petting her, telling her she was such a good girl, but she was far away behind her eyes. I told her she was the best thing to ever happen to me. I told her how much I loved her.

Two student vets came in. I begged them to look at Lucy. They said they were not allowed to without a teacher. They began to make small talk but I didn't want small talk, I just wanted a vet to look at Lucy. They said they heard I had been up to Reyhanlı and that I should be careful. They said Syria was too dangerous, and I might not make it back out alive. I said, I've thought about it long and hard, and if there is a small chance of helping so many people's lives then I was prepared to take the chance with my own life.

Suddenly, Lucy took in a breath and then made a strange exhaling rasp, like all the breath was leaving her. I ran around to her front, screaming for a vet. The room became crowded, with students all watching.

'Someone help Lucy! Please help Lucy…' I stopped screaming and whispered what a good girl she was. I heard myself ask, 'Why is she looking at me like that? What's wrong with her?'

No-one answered. No-one was allowed to give a diagnosis without a teacher present. Eventually a student held up her hands and with two fingers made an X sign.

What does that mean? Somewhere deep down I knew what it meant, but that couldn't be possible.

'What does X mean?' I shouted. Another student made a cutting motion across his throat.

She's dead? Lucy is dead. Someone nodded their head once. I repeated the words in my mind. Lucy is dead.

I grabbed her into me and my legs buckled, and I wailed. The students left the room. The receptionist came in and apologised that we were still waiting on vets to arrive.

I decided that there was no way this was going to be our last moment, with Lucy on a cold, steel table. I lifted her up, and the receptionist asked what I was doing. I'm going outside, I said. He told me no, I couldn't. I ignored him and carried Lucy out into the sunshine and across the road and sat on the grass under a massive tree. I buried my face in her fur and took a few deep breaths, trying to stop my tears. I told her she was such a good girl and I loved her and I thanked her. And then I promised her I would help all the other Lucys in Turkey.

The autopsy vet came over to us and said that they could do an autopsy for me. But I signalled I needed a few more minutes. I didn't want to get up from the grass. Because when I did, that was it; I would never have Lucy in my arms again.

I loved her so much. But I had to. I had to get up. I had to stand up and end our final moment. The vet was waiting.

When I finally stood up with Lucy in my arms, a quiet thought passed suddenly through my mind: I deserve unconditional love. I had no idea where it came from. I'd never had that thought before. But it was more than a thought. It was a belief from deep inside me – so strong, it was as if it had already existed within me.

During the autopsy, the students took me to a café to wait. The vet returned and showed me photos from the autopsy. She said she wanted to get toxicology tests done. They wanted to send Lucy's organs on an 11-hour bus ride to Ankara to get the tests done. I agreed but said there was no way I was letting her go on a bus by herself; that I would go too. They asked what they should do with her body, and I donated her body for research.

I walked out of the university covered in Lucy's blood but without Lucy. I went back to the flat. I looked at the blobs of black blood on the floor and went to the kitchen for a cloth and cleaned it up. Then I stood in the shower and I sobbed and sobbed.

Afterward, I packed everything up. I took my bicycle and gear to be stored and booked my ticket to Ankara. Then I went to the university.

They had packed Lucy's organs into a white polystyrene box with ice bags. I would have just enough time to get them to a freezer in Ankara. The student vet who had been closest to Lucy accompanied me as I walked out of the university with the box, and along the shop fronts that Lucy and I had passed every day.

The shopkeepers and café owners stepped out and looked confused, asking, 'Where's Lucy?' I looked down at the box, pleading with myself not to cry. I pointed to the box. She's dead,

I said. I saw on their faces looks of confusion, disbelief, sadness, and compassion.

I sat down in the café where she and I had sat every day. We put the box in an empty fridge in the café's kitchen and waited until it was time for the bus. It arrived at 8 p.m., and my vet friend explained the box to the driver. We placed the box underneath the bus, where the driver said it would be cooler.

I got on the bus and took my seat, and in the darkness, I cried and cried. I was back on my bed in foster care, screaming but not making a sound.

In Ankara I followed the directions I'd been given to the lab, which was closed when I arrived. The security guard told me to come back later, when it was open. I was numb and remained standing in the rain with Lucy's box. Perhaps feeling pity for me, the guard took me with him inside and unlocked a door so I could put Lucy's organs in a refrigerator. He then took me upstairs to the department to sit for an hour before the staff arrived. His kindness reminded me of all the good moments Turkish people had showed Lucy.

I sat in the waiting area, sometimes sobbing, sometimes just numb.

When the staff arrived, they called me over, and I watched as they took each of Lucy's body parts out of the box and recorded it on a list, which I then had to sign.

The manager, who spoke English, said he already knew from the autopsy photos that Lucy didn't die of poison, but he explained they would be doing tests on over 150 toxins as requested by Hatay University. He said they would examine everything and write a full report.

I thanked everyone, and then I went to the bus station and didn't know what to do. I couldn't face going back to Hatay to get my bike and trailer, so I caught a bus to the last place Lucy and I felt at home – Calis. I sent a message to my friend there, Brian, saying I'd arrive early the next morning and to make sure there was a bottle of wine. I arrived at 7.30 a.m., opened the bottle of wine and I drank it all, and then went to bed and cried myself to sleep.

CHAPTER 21

Lucy was gone, and in her place was overwhelming devastation. The words *Lucy's dead* swirled in my head as I tried to make sense of it. *Please come back, Lucy. Don't be gone.* But my beautiful girl was never coming back. The words I had repeated for months, 'You're a good girl, Lucy,' looped in my mind. The ache was terrible.

I wrote a Facebook post about her death:

Lucy's dead. She died on the last day of her 3-month quarantine period. Tomorrow she would have been free to go to the UK.

Heartbroken messages from Lucy's fans poured in. They had followed our journey and were grieving alongside me. Many made donations to local shelters in honour of Lucy; others sent gentle words that enveloped me in love and compassion, helping to pull me up from my sadness.

I grieved because I missed her. I grieved because I had failed her by not giving her the happy ever after I had promised. I grieved because maybe I could have done more somehow. My grief debilitated me. It would have been so easy to revert to my old ways of detachment, self-blame, and blocking out as I had with past traumas, but sharing Lucy with people around the world made this impossible; so instead, I grieved openly and cried and cried and cried.

Lucy had smashed the wall around my heart, and, now free of it, I never wanted to build that wall again, because it belonged to a life before Lucy. Like Lucy, I would operate from love instead of fear.

The autopsy showed Lucy had advanced heartworm, which in itself would be fatal, but what actually killed her was a gastric perforation from chronic gastrointestinal disease. Undoubtedly she had been in great pain, which grieved me anew.

It was months afterward when I was finally able to see past the sadness and guilt – that I realised that I had been Lucy's happy ever after. The epiphany brought with it a tremendous uplifting feeling of relief and joy. I recalled all the wonderful moments we had shared and how happy Lucy had been. When we first met, she had lived in fear, expecting to be hurt by humans, but by the time she died, that fear had evolved into love, with the expectation that people would love her, not hurt her. And she had loved us right back.

My friends say Lucy's death saved my life. I had been warned in the Syrian Revolution Command Centre that holding a British and Iranian passport meant I had no allies in Syria, and if caught by either side, the chances were high I'd be tortured and killed. I had been so affected by what I had witnessed at the border that I hadn't cared. But with Lucy's death, I was lost in grief and struggling to function, so I delayed my departure to the border. In that time, Syrian refugees fleeing the war began a mass migration into Europe, and Germany stepped forward and opened its borders, which opened up the overland route with little risk of death.

In the weeks that followed Lucy's death, I spent time visiting dog shelters to learn more about street animals. I had made a promise to Lucy and to myself that I would help the other Lucys in Turkey, and I knew that educating myself was fundamental to this. I also met with the chairman of the Animal Rights Charity in Istanbul. We discussed his ideas on neuter-and-release being a humane way of population control, and agreed that education was crucial in changing people's attitudes toward dogs and lessening harm from humans.

My Turkish visa was coming to an end. I took a 16-hour bus ride to Hatay, following the same roads Lucy and I had cycled. Memories flooded each twist and turn in the road. I collected my bike and trailer, and an hour later I had it on a bus back to Calis. There, I disconnected the bike from the trailer and loaned the trailer to Animal Aid, where it was used to feed the street cats and transport injured and sick street animals for veterinary care.

My passport had been posted to me in Hatay, but I didn't go straight back to Scotland. I left my bike and the trailer in Turkey because I couldn't bear cycling off without Lucy in the trailer. I caught a cheap flight to Iran and backpacked to the rice fields where my Iranian family originated. I found out my grandfather's brother's second wife (it being legal to have multiple wives in Iran) was still alive. I spent some time there and it was incredibly special. I was fascinated by life in the rice fields and loved helping the local women plant rice. For the first time in my life I was surrounded by people who had the same features as me. I had reconnected with another part of myself.

Then I flew back to Scotland. Most people in my life didn't know about my troubled past. I had been too ashamed to tell anyone, even friends I'd had for a decade. I began opening up about it and explained how my past and fear of abandonment had kept me at a distance. The most wonderful thing happened. My best friend became like a sister, and her whole family accepted me as their own. I spent Christmas Day with them, and we all sat in a circle on the floor, opening presents. I expected a little token gift so I wouldn't feel left out, but I was astounded to be given a stack of presents just like everyone else. I bit my lip and looked up at my family and said, 'I know I'm going to cry when I open my presents, but I want you to know it's tears of happiness.' I spent the next Christmas with an elderly gentleman, Jack, who was 75 years old and used to fix my bicycles. As usual, he would be spending Christmas Day alone, so I stayed with him and we shared a proper Christmas. He thanked me for the first Christmas dinner he had had in years. Our relationship, filled with the kind of father–daughter closeness I had always dreamed of, has grown into one of the most incredible, rewarding experiences of my life.

I also got in touch with my second cousins, and they enveloped me into their family as well. Gareth, Elaine, and I have become like family, too; my other home in the world is with them in Turkey, and I visit every chance I can. We walk along Calis Beach and I remember Lucy running and playing, and I smile as I whisper, *Thank you, Lucy.*

I wish I could say I had a happy ending with my mum, but I mourned once more as she said the words, 'It's over, we're finished.' But this time I was surrounded by people who loved me and got through it without shutting down and without breaking. The greatest thing about my life now is I'm not alone.

When I set out to cycle the world, I knew I was too damaged to love or be loved, but Lucy gave me back the Ishbel that I had been before the damage was fully done, and I'm not scared to love anymore. It feels good knowing I won't destroy future relationships because of my past.

I continue cycling the world and volunteering at rescue shelters and sterilisation projects, and I visit Scotland every year for a few months to spend time with my family.

It took me a long time, but when I was ready I collected Lucy's trailer in Calis, attached it to my bicycle, and began an animal rescue bike ride across Brazil.

To have so many people who love and care for me is something I only dreamed of before Lucy. Not only did she give me unconditional love, she gave me belonging, she gave me home, and most of all she gave me family.

Things don't always have the happy endings we want in life, but what's important is how we use these moments to shape our future for the better and make the world a better place.

Today, education programmes are gradually being rolled out across Turkey aimed at teaching the importance of neutering and in some parts of the country there are NGOs that feed street animals, work with communities and go into schools to teach students about the care and welfare of animals. There are some incredible acts of kindness towards animals by Turkish people, and as education improves, animal welfare will too.

Dear Lucy,

I love you so much. You're the best dog in the whole world and the greatest thing to ever happen to me. I miss you, and never a day passes when I don't think of you. I'm sorry you never got to live the happy ever after that I envisioned for you, but I know in my heart that I was your happy ever after. I only hope I gave to you even half of what you gave to me. You changed my life, Lucy, and I am incredibly grateful.

When our paths crossed, I was a human so damaged I was incapable of love. But you changed that. I have a home now, Lucy, and family. Real family who love and care for me. And you did that.

You are an amazing dog. People think I rescued you, but you rescued me too, Lucy and this book is my promise to you, to help your friends still on the streets.

There is no need to say goodbye because you are with me always in everything I do.

You're such a good girl, Lucy, and I love you with all my heart.

Thank you,
Ishbel xxx

HOW YOU CAN HELP

If Lucy's story speaks to you, there are ways you can help. Thousands of volunteers and organizations around the world are aiding the cause of animals, and I have selected two that are close to my heart. Meanwhile The Rees Foundation is a charity helping those who have experienced care. Their events have had an incredible impact on my life – and one of the results was writing this book.

LUCY'S LEGACY

This is a charity I began in Lucy's name, aimed at helping street dogs around the world. The organization focuses on education as well as frontline rescue efforts.

Lucylegacy.org

THE HARMONY FUND

This charity based in the United States supports frontline animal rescue groups around the world, with a particular focus on underfunded animal rescue squads in poor communities.

harmonyfund.org

REES FOUNDATION

The Care Leavers Foundation – supporting people who've been in care. One weekend of peer networking changed my life and my future.

Reesfoundation.org

NOTE FROM THE AUTHOR

For anyone considering bicycle touring, please do not be out off by any of the negative moments in this book. I have cycled 16 countries and Turkey is the only country where I received harassment from men.

So please JUST GO!

You'll have one of the most incredible journeys of your life!

Attitudes and understanding towards mental health have come on leaps and bounds from previous decades and my earlier experiences belong in an era lacking understanding, support or compassion. It's important not to judge anyone when they could be suffering from poor mental health – and that includes anyone in this book.

Most frontline animal rescue efforts are done by every-day people who simply can't stand by anymore and watch animals suffer around them, so they take action. Those rescuers have to deal every day with stress and anxiety. I have only compassion for everyone described here.

Cycling the world has taught me not to judge other countries negatively. Nineteenth-century Britain was very similar to contemporary Turkey in its treatment of animals. Turkey is at the same crossroads we once faced on how to manage the street animal population and improve animal welfare. Britain chose to kill street animals, on the premise that an animal without an owner had no right to life. Turkey is taking a profoundly different route and their laws state a street animal has the right to life, introducing a national neuter-and-return programme. If Turkey succeeds in their mission perhaps Britain shall learn from Turkey.

ACKNOWLEDGEMENTS

My first and biggest THANK YOU goes to the online World Bike Girl community. Thousands of miles separate us, yet you have been with me through the smiles, laughter and tears that such a life-changing journey brings. It's astonishing how much you've helped me; not only in my adventures but also in my personal growth and development. And of course, what I do with street dogs would not be possible without you and I am grateful every day.

A huge thank you to my agent, Jennifer Barclay, for being so amazing. I couldn't have wished for a better agent. And she has an awesome dog, Lisa!

Thank you to my publishers, Velo Press (USA) and Bradt Travel Guides (UK). It has been such an incredible and positive experience working with both. Special thanks to lead editor, Casey Blaine of Velo Press, whose guidance and encouragement were wonderful and who gave me many giggles as I perplexed her with my use of Scottish slang words such as numpty, scheme and dug – you did well, Casey!

This book wouldn't be possible without Frank Gilhooley, actor and script writer who asked to write the film script of my life. He was the first person I shared my full past with in detail and his support and encouragement ignited the strength and self-belief to write this book.

A very special thank you to my therapist Sena Moran LMHC, who helped me understand and process my past. THANK YOU!

Special thanks to: Elaine and Gareth Patten, the Holmes family, the Henderson family, the Rigley family, Rachel Nevaro, Eva Wiater, Brian Wright, Kathy Conner, Debbie Houston, Dales Cycles, Susan Brownlie, Intelligent Data Group, Simon Stanforth, Steve, Mags and Jo Hosier, Volkan Oklar, Scott Glasgow, Fiona Kidd & Mark Fallon, Sue Fisher and Darren Duffield, Ann and Tom Vance, Susan Rimmington, Zekeriya Kazanci, John and Linda Brett, Pauline and Andy Trent, Jane Akatay, Bulent Aksakal, David and Anne Marie Tomkins, Jack Clark, Elizabeth and Abigail, Kate and Charlie, James Scott and Glynn Woods.

ABOUT THE AUTHOR

Ishbel Rose Holmes, a.k.a. World Bike Girl, is a British-Iranian adventurer who is scared of spiders. In 2014, she set off to bicycle the world and has so far pedalled across 16 countries in Europe and South America. She cycles with a dog trailer that she uses to help injured cats and dogs get medical care and find homes. Before cycling the world, Ishbel was a velodrome sprinter for the Iranian National Women's Team, and she has also road raced extensively in the United Kingdom. Ishbel is devoted to the social, environmental, and health benefits of cycling. She gives talks all over the world about her adventures and street dogs, and is a motivational speaker, promoting the positive effects of adventure and the great outdoors on mental health and quality of life.

Ishbel is an avid wearer of socks with sandals – much to the dismay of her friends.

Connect with Ishbel online at:
www.worldbikegirl.com
www.ishbelholmes.com
Twitter/Facebook/Instagram: World Bike Girl